A Pedlar's Legacy

OVERLEAF **Founder of the business.**
Antonio Fattorini as a young man

A Pedlar's Legacy

The Origins and History of Empire Stores
1831 ~ 1981

by Patrick Beaver

HENRY MELLAND · London

First published in Great Britain
by Henry Melland Limited
23 Ridgmount Street, London WC1E 7AH
1981
for Empire Stores Limited
Bradford, West Yorkshire BD99 4XB

Designed by Norman Reynolds

ISBN 0 9500730 6 7

Set in 11/12 point Baskerville Medium
Printed in Great Britain by
Watmoughs Limited, Bradford

Contents

BY THE SAME AUTHOR

The Big Ship
The Crystal Palace
A History of Lighthouses
A History of Tunnels
The Wipers Times
Victorian Parlour Games for Today
The Spice of Life
Yes! We Have Some (The History of Fyffes)
I.N.I.T.I.A.L. (The Story of the Initial Group)
All About the Home (The Story of Addis Limited)

Acknowledgments

The author wishes to thank all those of Empire Stores and the Fattorini family who have given so much help in compiling this history; in particular he is indebted to Miss Julia Gray for invaluable assistance. Special thanks are also due to Mr Wilfred Fattorini of Skipton.

He is also grateful to Mrs Valerie Dyson of Bradford who most generously put at his disposal her excellent study in depth of the Fattorini family.[1] Without it the task of writing this book would have been far more difficult.

[1] *The Fattorini Family, and its Contribution to Mail Order Trading in the United Kingdom* (Bradford University, February 1977).

Foreword

by Joseph Fattorini

Photograph by Swaebe

I am writing from Zermatt, one of my two favourite places in the world; the other is Bellagio on Lake Como in Italy and strangely enough according to tradition that is where this saga begins. My only claim to write a prologue is that I am the oldest member of the family still associated with Empire Stores Limited, having been with it for over 50 years.

This is a story of legend and fact because the earliest days are based on stories handed down by word of mouth. For any business to survive through 150 years, six reigns, five generations and two world wars is quite an achievement and having been personally associated with the Company for one third of its history I will try to analyse why it succeeded.

The first hundred years were the years of the private entrepreneurs. The Industrial Revolution in England brought changes and opportunities which the early members of the family recognised, entered upon and developed, my great-grandfather Antonio being the first. Fortunes are made by seeing a need which is not being fulfilled and filling it.

I joined Empire Stores in autumn 1930 and was there for its Centenary. I was fortunate enough to enter at a time of slump when the working man was unable to pay cash not only for luxuries but also household necessities and clothing, and cheap credit by mail order fulfilled a need which had not been met. The last 50 years is largely the story of that development. Now at the end of my active business life, it is interesting to look back and try to see what one has learned and what experience may be of value in the future.

First of all, change is always going on, nothing is static and by recognising opportunities as they occur one can continue to develop both personally and commercially. Many things that appear to be new are not—just repetitions in different form. By coincidence, I started my business life in the slump of 1930 and at the end of my career we are now in the slump of 1980. I think this is a worse slump to contend with than that of the thirties. In 1930 at least there was no inflation, no high interest rates, and fewer industrial problems; but social security is a great deal better today.

Empire Stores is no longer a small business run by personal entrepreneurs but a large public company with a professional board on which some members of the family still serve. It is rather like a huge modern oil tanker compared with the privateer of the eighteenth century. It is a modern product in a modern age, run by modern management, in whom I have every confidence. I learnt in 1930 that at the bottom of the slump at least it can't get worse. And if a business is trimmed of all its frills it will be in shape to ride the tide of recovery which will come.

For Empire Stores, 1981 is the end of an era, but the next 50 years hold out challenges with computers, micro-chip technology and other scientific advances which will, in every way, equal the changes brought about by the industrial revolution.

I am too old to lead into this age but not too old to see its possibilities. I believe Empire Stores has a board trained for these changes. In the past the family always put the business first, believing rightly that if they did this it would prosper and they would prosper with it. It is the same for this board today. If they make Empire Stores their first consideration and are not deflected by external pressures, the Company will travel the path through its second century to the benefit of all those associated with it.

Introduction
Empire Stores and mail order

The background

There are relatively few firms in Britain today that can claim to have been founded during the reign of William IV. One of them is Empire Stores Limited, the well-known Bradford mail order company which now serves over two million customers in the United Kingdom alone. This company started its life as a small jewellery and fancy-goods shop that was opened in Leeds in 1831 by Antonio Fattorini, an enterprising young immigrant from northern Italy. During the one and a half centuries of its existence the firm has lived through seven reigns, four major wars and any number of economic crises: yet, throughout that long history, it has grown steadily while always adapting to continually changing social and industrial conditions.

On seeking the reasons why a particular retail business has survived and prospered for so long, while countless others have come and gone, it is important to examine, however briefly, the social and economic conditions that were operating at the time such a business was started, for those forces must necessarily have created a need for the firm's activities and given it an initial impetus.

Towards the end of the eighteenth century there occurred in England a great industrial growth and, through an improved general standard of health, a fall in the death rate and an increase in births. As a result the population graph soared upwards throughout the nineteenth century. This led to a steady economic expansion by simultaneously increasing production through extending the demand for goods and supplying the labour for producing them. This in turn brought about a sharp increase in the living standards of the majority of working people and an ever-increasing

Empire Stores
Autumn·Winter 1981

Jubilee
Celebration
Year
1831 1981

demand for goods at prices they could afford. The result of this demand was a revolution in the retail industry. The patterns of the distribution of goods that had remained unchanged since the middle ages (travelling pedlars, weekly markets and annual fairs) evolved to become the modern system of retailing with its shops and department stores, wholesale houses, brand names and nationwide distribution.

The story of Empire Stores is in itself a history of that development in marketing patterns, for the company has its origins in the travelling pedlar, the market and the fair. From those humble beginnings the firm has developed on lines that parallel the unprecedented social and industrial changes of the last 150 years. It is now one of the biggest and most modern retailing organisations in the country. This steady growth was achieved through the consistent following of a policy of making goods available to working people at a low profit and maintaining a high turnover by so doing. This was the strategy of Antonio Fattorini when he started the business in 1831; it was the firm's policy when it first entered the mail order business, and it is the policy that Empire Stores follows today.

What is mail order?

In short, mail order is a commercial retail enterprise carried on mainly by means of the mail, whereby customers order, from illustrated catalogues sent to them twice a year by post, general merchandise of every description and receive their orders by parcel post, rail or road. All goods are sent to the customer on an 'approval' basis and on a system of extended credit.

This kind of retail business (which took concrete form in the USA in about 1872) has been established in Britain for some 80 years but it is only since the end of the last war that it has grown to its present great size and importance. It is undisputed that this still-continuing growth has improved the standards of living for millions of people. The chief reason for this is that a number of economic factors enable the mail order firms to supply first-class merchandise to their customers on advantageous, convenient terms and still at competitive retail prices. The first great economy is the elimination of a middleman, for almost without exception mail order houses buy from the factory and sell direct to the consumer. The big firms

LEFT **Cover of Autumn–Winter catalogue 1981**

buy in vast quantities and can place large orders with factories at a time when the latter would otherwise be slack; not infrequently a mail order house will take over almost the entire output of a manufacturer. Then again, because they buy for a whole 'season' of six months they can combat inflation by forward purchasing.

In operating methods also great economies are brought about, especially in the handling, packing and dispatching of merchandise. While orders to a mail order house correspond to customers shopping in a retail store, mail order has a great advantage in that the number of orders (or customers) at any given time can be controlled. There is no lost effort or unnecessary cost anywhere, for there are no idle shop assistants waiting for customers nor taking time to explain, handle or sell; instead there is a steady, uninterrupted flow of business which is the same at nine o'clock in the morning as it is at any other time of day, and the rush hours and slack periods experienced by retail shops are eliminated.

In recent years the retail shop industry in its various forms ('hypermarket', 'supermarket' and 'multiple') has also expanded, and yet in spite of this more and more people are turning to mail order. The ease of ordering, the convenience of having goods delivered, the extended credit, all these factors help to explain the growing popularity of mail order. Today in Britain almost 20 million people use the system and they make an estimated half million purchases a day.

The agent

It may be said that every time a woman has to take a bus ride to go shopping, or has to park her car a mile or so away from her favourite department store, or drag her complaining children around a shopping centre in the rain; every time she is persuaded to buy something she does not really want or spend more money than she had intended, this woman becomes a potential customer of Empire Stores. And if she does become a customer she will receive a catalogue offering her in words and pictures everything that she would expect to find in a department store. Then at her leisure and in the comfort of her home she can browse through nearly a thousand pages of clothing, footwear, furniture, gardening and motoring requisites, television and radio sets, records, musical instruments, toys, sporting and holiday goods, food, wine, spirits and thousands of other things all available on free, open credit and delivered to her door on two weeks' approval. And she need not confine the catalogue to her own requirements but may, if she wishes, act as a part-time agent for the firm, taking orders from her friends and neighbours, delivering the goods to them and collecting the money. For her efforts she will receive 10 per cent of the total sum of her business. As far as Empire Stores is concerned she will also be acting as a highly efficient means of credit control, for it takes a tough customer to bilk her neighbour.

But basically mail order succeeds because it fills a need. Consumers want to be informed about new products, they want to be sure they will get their money's worth, they want to buy things to make life easier, richer and more pleasant. Mail order gives them the opportunity to fill all these wants easily and economically.

Today Empire Stores deals with some 400,000 part-time agents, each of whom serves an average of five customers and handles a turnover of £350 a year. Between them they send to the Bradford head office a total of over six million orders a year which together consist of more than 16 million items. Trading on this vast scale is difficult to reconcile with the one-man business that began it all in 1831, yet the firm's actual origins are even humbler and older than this. To examine them we must go back to the small, remote village of Bellagio in northern Italy in the year of the battle of Waterloo.

PART I
The Origins
1815–1910

Lombardy

Antonio Fattorini was born in 1797 in the typically picturesque Lombard village of Bellagio. It is situated on a promontory of Lake Como, 15 miles north of the city of Como; its chief industry is olive-wood carving.

Nothing is known about Antonio Fattorini's parentage and early life except that he grew up in times that were troubled for Europe generally and momentous for Italy and Lombardy in particular. In the year that preceded Antonio's birth, Napoleon Bonaparte attacked Italy and, after a brilliant four week campaign that included several of his most famous victories, entered Milan in triumph as the conqueror of all Lombardy and Piedmont, thus temporarily ending the centuries-old Austrian domination of the region. With the ancient iron crown of the Lombard kings, Napoleon was made king of all Italy in 1805. He held that exalted office until 1812 when, after the destruction of the French army in the snows of Russia, he lost all his foreign territories and, in 1814, abdicated and was exiled to the Isle of Elba. During that year the Austrians reconquered most of northern Italy and reoccupied Lombardy. In 1815 Napoleon left Elba and established himself at Fontainbleau where he was joined by the French army. The scene was then set for the decisive conflict at Waterloo, and it is at that point in history that we first hear of Antonio Fattorini.

An early 19th century pedlar
Mansell collection

Bellagio on Lake Como, the birth-place of Antonio Fattorini
Italian State Tourist Office

'I will get an old gun'

By an instrument signed in April 1815 the Austrian territories in northern Italy were formed into the kingdom of Lombardo-Venetia which, although an integral part of the Austrian Empire, was to enjoy a separate administration, something the Lombards had not had for centuries. Although they hated the Austrians, the Lombard people were not prepared to allow Napoleon to rob them of their new-found autonomy should he become victor in Europe. It was this that prompted many young men of Lombardy to join the British and Prussian armies that were gathering to give battle to the

French. Among them was the 18 year old Antonio Fattorini who, together with a band of other young patriots, made his way to join the Duke of Wellington's army some 700 miles away. The story of his departure for the war was recorded years later by his son Frank.

> My father used to tell me about his experiences and said that one day in 1815 he was up in a tree gathering some mulberry leaves to feed the silkworms when a lot of young men came through the village. He asked them where they were going and they said they were going to fight Napoleon. 'Well,' he says, 'I can go with you. I will go and get an old gun.'

The party left Italy by way of the St Gotthard Pass, climbing to its 6,000-foot summit on the mule track which was then the only route. From there they made their way through Switzerland into Germany and then, via Strasbourg and Nancy, to Luxembourg on the way to the British army's cantonments near Brussels. But before the band reached their destination the battle of Waterloo had been fought and the French army defeated. When the news of the battle and its outcome reached Antonio and his friends some turned back for home but seven decided to make for England. They were all young men eager for experience and adventure and aware of the opportunities that existed in the 'workshop of the world'. They also knew that the British authorities were actively encouraging young Italians, Swiss and other Europeans to emigrate to Britain.

On landing in England the seven men made their several ways to the north, probably because friends and relations had already settled there, for the prosperity of the industrial north had for years been a strong attraction to European immigrants. Of the seven it is known that one, Vassell, made for Scarborough; another, Catanes, settled in Leeds; Barnasconi went to Halifax; Carsatel and Opaduzzi made their homes in Manchester, where the latter went into business as a maker of looking glasses. Antonio Fattorini went to Dewsbury, then a town of 8,272 people. We do not know what led Antonio to choose Dewsbury, and whether or not, when making his choice, he was aware that the town was a centre for the pedlars, hawkers and travelling packmen then working the northern counties. It was in Dewsbury that these itinerant traders stocked up for the journeys that took them from place to place selling their goods at markets and fairs. We do know that within five years of his arrival in England, Antonio Fattorini was in business on his own account as a travelling packman.

19th century English country fair
Mansell collection

Pedlars and packmen

Nowadays people think of their standard of living in terms of getting money and spending it, whereas when Antonio Fattorini first took to the road most people were to a great extent self-sufficient in food, fuel and even clothing. They thought only incidentally of the things they could buy with money, and these were generally limited to items requiring special skills and equipment for their manufacture, such as pots, pans, tools and 'luxury goods'. The last category included many articles that we take for granted today, such as tableware, cutlery and items of personal adornment. For all these the country dweller relied mainly on the weekly town market and the annual or semi-annual fair. To the markets and fairs came the packmen with loaded mules or donkeys, offering domestic metalware, knives and forks, plates and dishes, cheap watches and jewellery, combs, penknives, clocks, lamps, china vases, bowls and other household ornaments, needles, pins, ribbons, bows, boots, shoes and many other things.

This type of itinerant distribution was characterised by a massive substitution of labour for capital. Typically, the pedlars and packmen held very small stocks, enough perhaps for a week's trading. They sometimes bought direct from manufacturers, but as often obtained supplies at a discount from shops in the larger towns. This was good business for the shopkeepers as it was sometimes the only way they could reach country-dwelling workers. Many a large wholesale concern was built up from a shop through trading with travelling dealers: collectively their turnover was big.

Sometime before 1820 Antonio Fattorini married an English girl named Maria. Then, having amassed a working capital of about £100, he obtained the required backing of 'two respectable people and one clergyman', and applied for and was granted a pedlar's licence. This cost him £4 a year plus an additional £4 licence fee for the donkey that carried the pack. Thus equipped he toured the countryside as a 'travelling jeweller', visiting rural markets and fairs on a rota system for six days each week, selling cheap jewellery, looking glasses, barometers, watches, scissors, razors and penknives.

During those early days Antonio saw little of his wife and the young son (also Antonio) the couple then had, for his visits to the various markets and fairs involved considerable travelling. It is doubtful whether he returned home more than once a week, and then probably on Saturdays to replenish his stock and spend Sundays with his family. Most nights were spent on the road, sleeping in fields on fine nights and cooking for himself over a camp fire or, in bad weather, staying at cheap wayside inns. Some account of the long distances travelled by the pedlars of those days was recorded by William Green, a London-based packman who was active on the road between 1825 and 1850.

> I used to go out with a lot of goods on the Wednesday to Romford market, on Thursday to Bishops Stortford, Friday to Chelmsford, Saturday to Colchester, Wednesday to Bury St Edmunds, Thursday to Diss and on Saturday to Norwich.

William Green also states that the roads were dangerous to travel in those days and that the packmen tended to move in groups of three or more; even then they were usually armed. It is not difficult to picture Antonio Fattorini, alone or with a couple of companions, plodding with his loaded donkey along the miles of empty roads and lanes of rural England, passing only an occasional farm or market wagon, dogcart, horseman or rustic wayfarer. There must have been times when, trudging through the wind, rain or snow of the northern English winter, he thought wistfully of the warm plains of Lombardy; and there must have been days of bright blue skies and shining sun when he sang aloud the old songs of his homeland.

The shopping revolution

An industrious packman with a shrewd judgment of his markets, a strong personality and a bright, persuasive line of patter could make a good living in the heyday of country fairs and markets. Antonio possessed all these attributes and, dealing as he did with the more expensive kinds of merchandise, he could take as much as £40 on the first day of a large fair, a sum that then represented a year's wages of an agricultural worker. But by the time Antonio had got his travelling business into full stride, as it were, the age of the market and fair was in decline, for the shopping methods of the ordinary people were undergoing a rapid change.

From the late eighteenth century through to the nineteenth, personal, local and regional self-sufficiency in England began to break down as the factory system developed and the growing population required more efficient distribution services. The country fairs were the first to suffer in the face of these changes. As an exchange mechanism they had, for centuries, operated usefully and economically in predominantly rural societies characterised by slow communications and a low level of material demand. But fairs could not compete as part of a distribution system in an urban, industrialised society: by 1850 they had lost their marketing function altogether and, where they were not abolished, became purely pleasure fairs. The effect of this on the itinerant salesmen was serious, for the fairs represented a good proportion of their trade. In his book *On Commerce* (London, 1833) the British economist J. R. McCulloch wrote:

> Pedlars were at one time very common but since shops, for the sale of almost every sort of produce, have been opened in every considerable village throughout Britain their numbers have been greatly diminished.

There can be no doubt that Antonio Fattorini was early aware of the serious decline in the functions of the fair and travelling pedlar; he was also aware of the corresponding growth of town markets upon which an increasing proportion of the retail trade was concentrating. From 1800 onwards those markets had grown both in size and number, and as they did laws were passed by parliament giving local authorities powers to improve conditions and facilities in public market-places. As a result a new type of market came into being with covered pavements for stalls and shoppers, built-in shops, toilet facilities, fresh-water pumps and gas illumination. The first of these markets was opened in Liverpool in 1822; it was so successful that it was copied in towns and villages all over the country. With their high concentration of traders, they offered a range of merchandise to which the country markets could not even aspire, and on market days shoppers came by foot or by cart from miles around. Seeing this trend quickening through the 1820s, Antonio Fattorini decided to look about for a permanent base for his business.

Leeds market

In 1827 two markets were built and opened in Leeds, both by private enterprise. The larger of these was the Central Market situated on the corner of Duncan Street and Call Lane, and the other, the Briggate Market, between Briggate and Vicar Lane. The latter was for the 'better class' trade and had covered 'carriage roads' running between the shops and stalls. The opening of these markets so near to his home in Dewsbury presented Antonio Fattorini with the opportunity for which he had been waiting and so, with his wife and son, he went to Leeds and settled at 1 Upton's Yard, off Briggate. At the larger, more popular market Antonio established his first permanent trading site by renting a stall at 1s. 3d a day and stocking it with his usual range of cheap jewellery and fancy goods. Incongruously, one might think, he augmented this stock with a variety of more prosaic items, such as pots, pans, boots and knee-pads. The stall occupied Antonio on the two market days; on the other days he returned to the road, working the smaller markets in country towns. The necessity for his presence in the Central Market on two days a week prevented him from travelling as far afield as he used to do.

The year following the establishment of the stall in Leeds saw the birth of Antonio's second son, Innocent. As he was the first child to

Central Market, Leeds, where Antonio rented his first stall
By courtesy of Leeds City Libraries

be born to a trader in the Central Market since it opened there was (in Antonio's words) 'some jollification on account of it' among the stallholders.

The first shop

By 1830 the Fattorinis had three sons and during the following year the family moved to a larger house at 4 Turk's Head Yard, which was also off Briggate. Antonio, at the age of 33, was now a prosperous but hard-working, ambitious tradesman seeking ways to further increase his income while still, perhaps, being able to spend more time at home with his wife and sons. Therefore in 1831 he took the important step of giving up the stall in the Central Market and taking a lease at £18 a year of a small lock-up shop in the 'bazaar' section of the Briggate Market. This bazaar was a long balcony on the inside of the market building, lined with a number of small shops which sold jewellery, plate, china, glass and fancy goods. These shops were a particular attraction to the working people of Leeds for the purchase of their more fanciful requirements.

On moving into the shop Antonio gave up the domestic and hardware side of his business for, with the security of dealing *within* a building for the first time and from behind a counter he realised his ambition of selling 'real' jewellery, plate and good quality glassware. But nevertheless he took good care to confine his trade to the lower end of this market, for he knew his customers from experience and was aware that his success up to then was founded on low profits and high turnover.

It is an interesting fact that many great and well-known retail stores of today started business in market 'bazaars'. Kendal Milne, for example, started as the Manchester Bazaar, and Marks & Spencers as the Penny Bazaar in Leeds in 1884. In opening his small lock-up shop on the balcony of a Leeds market in 1831, Antonio Fattorini laid the foundation of the multi-million pound trading company that is Empire Stores today.

Fattorini's Oriental Salon

The development of retailing in Britain during the nineteenth century was as relevant to the evolution of society as the Industrial Revolution that preceded it. As the fear of hunger receded, and the general standard of living steadily improved, the increasing number and variety of shops reflected and assisted the changing economy. The market in luxury goods, especially, grew during this time, for it was a time when a prosperous working class was endeavouring to possess some of the trappings of the better off. This was the demand that Antonio Fattorini was able to satisfy from his shop during the city's two market days. As before, he continued to spend the remainder of the week trading at neighbouring markets.

One of the places on Antonio's itinerary was the small market town of Harrogate. It was described in a contemporary directory as a town '. . . celebrated for its *sulphurous and chalybeate springs*, one of the most fashionable watering places in the North of England . . . It occupies an elevated and salubrious situation $15\frac{1}{2}$ miles N. of Leeds'. The iron-impregnated waters of Harrogate were discovered in 1831 and the town developed into a prosperous spa and middle-

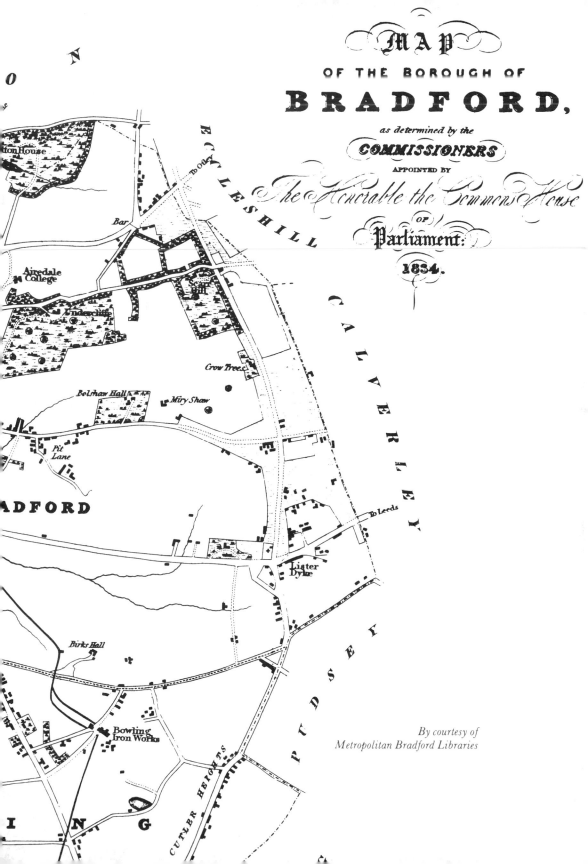

MAP
OF THE BOROUGH OF
BRADFORD,
as determined by the
COMMISSIONERS
APPOINTED BY
The Honorable the Commons House
OF
Parliament:
1834.

N

ton House

Bar

Airedale College

Scarr Hill

Undercliffe

ECCLESHILL

CALVERLEY

Crow Trees

Bolshaw Hall

Miry Shaw

Pit Lane

RADFORD

To Leeds

Lister Dyke

Birks Hall

PUDSEY

Bowling Iron Works

CUTLER HEIGHTS

I   N   G

class summer resort. In the early 1840s two fashionable London stores, Marshall & Snelgrove and Debenhams, opened branches in Harrogate, a development that was noted by Antonio Fattorini. Consequently, in 1841, he opened a branch of his jewellery and fancy-goods business in the town at 14 Regent's Parade; he described it as a 'fancy repository' and advertised it as 'Fattorini's Oriental Salon'. As the new shop opened six days a week Antonio moved his home to Harrogate to be near it, although he returned to Leeds twice a week to run the bazaar business. On those days the Oriental Salon was left to the management of his wife and eldest son. Over the following four years the Harrogate shop prospered. Then, in 1846, Antonio put its management entirely into the hands of the younger Antonio and moved with the rest of his family to Bradford, there to establish another, far larger, branch of the business.

Starting at Bradford

Antonio's choice of Bradford for his new venture was a shrewd one. The town was the centre and principal market for worsted manufacture and there were thriving coal, iron and stone industries in the surrounding districts. It had recently been connected with the Leeds-Liverpool canal and to the railway system. All the town's industries were rapidly expanding and with them Bradford's population, which already had grown from 6,400 in 1801 to 34,500 in 1831. The total population of the entire Bradford district was then some 70,000, and still increasing. It was this rapid growth in population and prosperity that brought Antonio Fattorini to the town, for a personal survey he had previously carried out showed there was a need for another jeweller's shop in Bradford as there were only five others—and this in a town that had 86 butchers' shops and 160 public houses. The shop chosen by Antonio for the new branch was a commodious two-storey building at 28 Kirkgate on the corner of Cheapside. By then Antonio had seven sons, and aided by one of them, Edward, he transformed the empty rambling building into a smart modern jewellery and silversmith's shop which within a few years became famous in Bradford and beyond as Fattorini & Sons. Because of the range, quality and, not least, price of its goods its reputation spread, for the low-profit margin policy was strictly adhered to. When the business was running smoothly, the shop in Leeds market was closed. Antonio then took life a little easier, leaving the running of the Bradford shop mainly in the hands of Edward, who lived above it with his wife and shop assistants.

Skipton

During the year in which the Bradford shop was opened yet another branch of the Fattorini family business was started. This, in the historic town of Skipton, some 20 miles from Bradford, was established by Antonio's son Innocent, then a young man of 18 who had recently completed an apprenticeship as a watchmaker and jeweller. Innocent was helped in starting the business by a friend of the family, Baldisaro Porri, who also ran a jewellery shop in Skipton. Born in 1803, Porri arrived in Britain from Italy at about the same time as Antonio Fattorini. In 1827 he opened a small business as a jeweller and optician in Skipton's Market Street. During the following years he probably travelled as a packman to neighbouring markets and fairs for, in 1830, one 'Benj. Perri' is recorded as trading in the Market Place, Leeds, as an 'Optician, Jeweller and Umbrella Manufacturer'.[1] It will be remembered that Antonio Fattorini was trading in Leeds market at that time and it is likely that he and Porri became acquainted there. The relationship between the two families, whether through business, nationality or religion, was a close one and it was sealed in 1860 by the marriage of Innocent to Porri's daughter, Mary Jane. The newly wed couple made their home above Innocent's shop at 19 Otley Street (then called New Street), Skipton. Then, in 1864, they moved both shop and home to handsome new premises that had been purpose built for them by Baldisaro Porri on the corner of High Street and Newmarket Street. For the next 75 years this building was known locally as Fattorini's Corner. The shop was described as one which '. . . greatly improved the architectural appearance . . . at a time when shops were small and antiquated looking, and building enterprise in Skipton was at a standstill'.[2] From that time the business prospered and, although it was independent of the

---

[1] *The mis-spelling of Baldisaro Porri's name was probably an attempt to anglicise it, for there was a 'Buy British' campaign at the time. It is unlikely that a market stallholder would have been an umbrella manufacturer in the conventional sense of the term. Porri was probably a 'mush faker', that is, a man skilled at assembling complete umbrellas from bits and pieces of old discarded ones and selling them for about 2s. od apiece. Mush=mushroom (umbrella); faker=maker.*

[2] *The Craven Herald & Pioneer, 1888.*

Cases of Electro-plate
DESSERT
KNIVES & FORKS
Containing 12 pairs,
£3, £3 15s. to £5;
Ditto with Ivory handles,
£3 10s. to £5;
Ditto with Pearl handles,
£4, £5, to £8;
Cases of Solid Silver
Dessert
KNIVES AND FORKS
Containing 12 pairs,
£10, £12, and £14

Fish Eating Knives and Forks, in cases containing 12 pairs, electro-plated handles, £3 15s., £4 10s., and £5 10s.
Ditto, ivory handles, £5, £6, and £7 the case of 12 pairs
Ditto, pearl handles, £6, £7, and £9 the case of 12 pairs

The knives may be had without the forks, at a little over half the price.

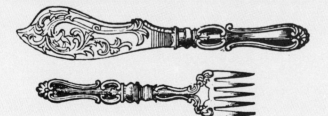

FISH CARVERS,
IN MOROCCO CASE,
ELECTRO-PLATE,
15s. to 40s.

Solid Silver Fish Carvers, £4 to £7, with Silver, Ivory, and Pearl Handles.

Cake Knife and Fork, in case, Electro-plate, 10s., 15s., and 20s.
Cake Knife and Fork, in case, Solid Silver, 35s., 40s., and 50s.
Butter Knives, in Solid Silver, from 6s. 6d. each
Pickle Forks, in Solid Silver, from 2s. 6d. each
Ladies' Card Cases, in Solid Silver, 33s.
Fruit Spoons, Solid Silver, 30s. to 40s. each
Napkin Rings, Electro-plate, from 3s.
Napkin Rings, Solid Silver, 7s. 9d. to 10s. 6d.
Mustard Pots, Electro-plate, 5s. to 15s.
Mustard Pots, Solid Silver, 40s. to 70s.

Silver goods repaired and re-polished. Old plated goods re-plated equal to new

SILVER and ELECTRO-PLATE—*continued*.

CAKE BASKETS

ELECTRO-PLATED,
20s., 30s., 40s., up to £4.

SOLID SILVER

CAKE BASKETS,

£12 to £18.

THE NEW BISCUIT BOXES IN EVERY VARIETY,
From 20s., 30s., 40s., to 60s.

TOAST RACKS,

ELECTRO-PLATE,

7s. 6d. to 18s.

SOLID SILVER,

£6 to £9.

BEDROOM CANDLESTICKS

In a great variety of patterns,
Electro-plate, 7s. 6d., 10s., and
12s. 6d.

TABLE CANDLESTICKS,

All sizes, 20s., 25s., to 30s. the pair.

Sauce Boats, 15s., 20s., and 25s.
Hot-water Dishes, for chops, bacon, or toasted cheese, £2 to £3.
Vegetable Dishes with 3 divisions, hot-water part and loose handle, £3 10.
Entrée or Corner Dishes, with covers, £10 to £15 the set of four—the
    handles take off to form 8 dishes.
Salvers from 20s. to 60s., according to size.
Salvers in Solid Silver commencing at 8 guineas.

Our own real Vienna Regulators,

which are acknowledged by the largest Clock Merchants
and Manufacturers in the world to be the best time
keepers ever produced.

Vienna Regulators in every
    variety, from
    20s. to £5 5s. 0d. each.

Fine Walnut Regulators same
    AS THIS ILLUSTRATION 52½
    inches long, 7 inch dial
        3 3 0

Ditto, striking hours
    and half-hours... 3 15 6

Other styles of Regulators
    from 1 15 0

Striking from ... 2 7 6

As the movements are
interchangeable, silent ones
can be changed for striking.

**EXTRA LARGE
SIZE.**

Our Greenwich Regulators
made by the maker of
our Vienna Regulators,
70 inches long, 10-inch
dial 5 5 0

Ditto, in Finest Burr
Walnut 6 6 0

Other styles up to 50 0 0

They have true seconds
pendulums, and are used in
the largest Watch Manufac-
tories in England for timing
the most expensive watches.

*We are the Sole Agents for these Clocks in the North of England. They
are the finest Timekeepers the world can produce, and are made by the maker
who took the HIGHEST PRIZE ever given to any Clock Manufacturer. Warranted
for Five Years. Illustrated Lists sent on application.*

SILVER and ELECTRO-PLATE—*continued*.

FLOWER STANDS

AND

VASES,

IN MANY BEAUTIFUL DESIGNS,

10s. to 50s.

Selection from
Fattorini catalogues
in the 1860s,
with Innocent's
introduction RIGHT

*In presenting to the public this Cata=
logue, Mr. Fattorini begs to thank his
many friends and patrons for the very
liberal patronage he has received since the
opening of his new shop, and also to in=
form them that the stock has lately been
enriched with a great variety of new
goods, an inspection of which is respect=
fully solicited.*

*Every article is marked in plain
figures, the lowest price.*

*Anything which may be purchased not
being satisfactory will be readily exchanged
or the money returned.*

*Orders by post receive careful and im=
mediate attention.*

*Mr. Fattorini is always at home on Mondays and
Saturdays; on other days he is uncertain, owing to his
travelling engagements.*

Bradford firm, it co-operated with the other Fattorini shops in the matter of bulk buying and advertising. The subsequent history of the Skipton firm is remarkably similar to that of Bradford's. In 1911 it started a mail order business which, under the name of National Direct Supply Stores, soon outgrew the shop business. Then, during the same period, it developed a trophy and regalia manufactory in Birmingham (as did the Bradford firm). During the 1930s the Skipton Fattorinis turned their entire attention to mail order and became one of the leaders in the industry. Eventually the firm was merged with the mail order company of John Myers and Company Limited.

Watches and clocks

In 1852 another Fattorini came into the Bradford firm: John, Antonio's youngest son, had finished a five-year apprenticeship with Richard Heselwood, a watchmaker and jeweller of Blake Street in the city of York. Having developed a particular aptitude and liking for the trade of horology, John entered the family firm as

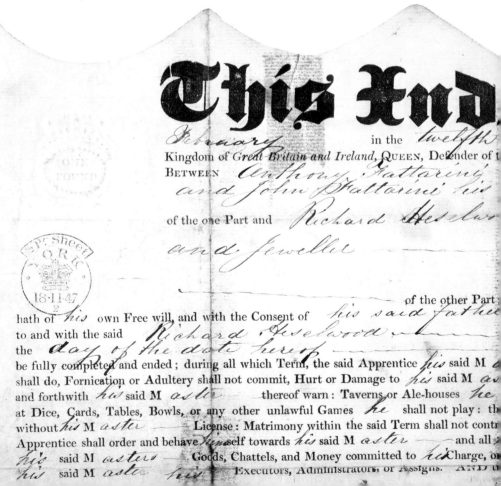

manager of the watch and clock repairing department, which by that time occupied an entire floor of the Kirkgate shop. John Fattorini however was not only a clever watchmaker but an astute businessman whose acumen and energies were to have far-reaching effects on the company's future. It was he who took the first step on the road that was eventually to lead the firm into mail order. Referring to John's early days in Bradford, his brother Frank (speaking many years later) said of him, '. . . at that time, about the early fifties, there was not a working man in Bradford who had a watch in his pocket and John saw it'.

But John had also seen the working man's *need* to have a watch in his pocket, for the industrialised society of the mid-nineteenth century had made people far more time-conscious than they had ever been before. The chime of the churchtower clock, indicating only approximately the hour of day or night, was no longer

John Fattorini's Indenture to Richard Heselwood,
watchmaker and jeweller of York

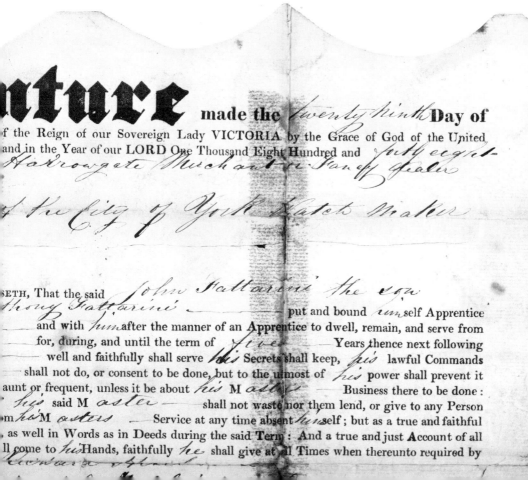

adequate. Factory and office demanded punctuality, as did the railways which were rapidly creating the commuter society. The pocket watch and domestic clock were becoming essentials rather than luxuries and, in obedience to the law that links necessity with invention, the mass production of watches was started in 1838 by the American firm of Henry Picton. Early in 1853 the American Waltham Watch Company of Boston began producing in large quantities watches cased in a variety of metals ranging from steel to silver and gold. The elegant Waltham watches differed little in form from the handmade variety but the method of production caused an enormous revolution in the price, for whereas the hand-crafted article cost several guineas, an accurate reliable, factory-made Waltham watch in a silver case could be bought retail for as little as a pound. John Fattorini was aware of the availability of these cheap but good watches; he was aware of the need for them, too; but he also knew that they were out of the reach of the lowest-paid workers to whom a pound represented a full week's wages. The problem (and John's answer to it) was thoroughly discussed and considered by all members of the Fattorini family then engaged in the business: the result was the formation of the first Fattorini Watch Clubs.

The purchasing clubs

At that time all three Fattorini jeweller's shops were giving limited credit without interest and over a relatively short period to customers of standing. The plan then was to introduce a system of credit which would enable working people with little or no creditworthiness to buy watches and clocks without risk of bad debts to the firm. This club system was both simple and ingenious. Each working in his own area, John, Edward, Innocent and the younger Antonio promoted and organised clubs, the members of which agreed to meet once a week at their local public house for the purpose of subscribing 6d a head into a common fund for a period of 50 weeks. Each club was properly constituted with a committee, chairman and treasurer. When a sum of £1. 5s had accumulated it was sent to one of the Fattorini shops for the purchase of a silver pocket watch. A discount was given by the shop and this was put into the club's social fund. The watch was then balloted (or raffled) and the winner continued his subscriptions until the end of

RIGHT **A Fattorini Watch Club catalogue 1875**

32

FATTORINI'S
FOURTH WATCH CLUB
FOR CARLETON.

As the third Club has now expired, having given every satisfaction, it is the wish of several of the old members to commence a FOURTH ONE.

THE

FIRST MEETING

WILL TAKE PLACE

On FRIDAY Evening, December 31st, 1875,

AT EIGHT O'CLOCK,

At Mrs. ELLISON'S, Swan Inn, Carleton,

When a committee will be chosen for the management of the Club ; also samples of Watches, Jewellery, &c., will be shown.

Persons desirous of obtaining information respecting the principles of the Club and the great advantages to be derived by the members, are requested to attend.

LIST OF ARTICLES SUPPLIED TO THE CLUB:—

Gold Watches ....£3 to £25	Tea Spoons....................from 1/6 half dozen
Silver Watches ....£1 1s. to £6 6s.	Table Spoons ....from 5/6 half dozen
Gold Albert Chains ....£1 10s. to £15	Dessert Spoons ....from 3/6 half dozen
Clocks of all kinds ....3/6 to £10	Ladies' Bags ....from 3/6
Wedding Rings ....7/6 to £2	Ladies' Work Boxes...................2/- to 40/-
Cruet Frames ... . 8/- to £5	Writing Desks ....3/6 to 40/-
Knives and Forks........from 3/6 half dozen.	HAIR BRUSHES & COMBS of all kinds
Britannia Metal Tea Pots ....3/- to 14/-	JET GOODS of every description
Britannia Metal Coffee Pots ....5/- to 14/-	SEWING MACHINES OF ANY MAKE.

Printed at Edmondson and Co.'s Steam Printing Works, High-street, Skipton.

the 50-week period. The process was repeated weekly until all the members had received their watches. This system of free credit was self-financing and without risk to the firm, for all risks of bad debts were borne collectively by the club members who, through their committee, were able to exclude bad payers from membership.

These watch clubs, with their easily available interest-free credit, were a success from the beginning, and as the paying of the weekly subscription became an occasion for meeting friends and neighbours and having a glass of beer they developed into valued social institutions. Thus, when all members had received watches, each club started another round of activity, this time for a watch chain perhaps, or a chiming clock or a set of cutlery. Eventually members were paying between 6d and 2s. od a week for 50 weeks against 'shares' of between £1. 5s and £5, and instead of a draw for a particular article it was made for a cheque that could be spent at a Fattorini shop only. The club imposed fines on any members late with their subscriptions, and this money, together with the discounts allowed on goods supplied, was used to provide a supper to the members at the end of each 50-week period. If the club was at any distance from the organising shop (as many were) the exchange of cheques for goods was done by post, and for this

General view of Bradford c1860
By courtesy of Metropolitan Bradford Libraries

purpose the firm issued catalogues. By so doing it instituted a mail order business which, based on free credit and discount (or commission), was in essence the same as it is today. A Fattorini Club catalogue has survived and it gives the rules for managing the club.

---

1) The Club shall be managed by a Secretary, Treasurer and Committee of seven members, three of whom shall form a quorum, and the shares will be of the value of £2. 10s, £3. 15s and £5. Half shares, £1. 5s.

2) Every member shall pay a weekly subscription of 6d, 1s, 1s. 6d or 2s according to the value of his share.

3) If any member allows his subscription to be in arrears for over four weeks, he shall be fined fourpence, or one penny for every week he is in arrears.

4) A ballot will take place every fourth week, for determining who shall take the next share and each member on taking his share shall pay sixpence, which together with all the fines, shall go to a fund for providing a supper, or otherwise disposed of as members may agree upon expiration of the club and Mr Fattorini will provide a sum equal in amount to the fund for the same purpose.

5) Any person desirous of becoming a member of this club after it shall have been established, may do so on payment of the value of his subscriptions from the commencement up to the time of his entrance.

6) When a member draws his share he shall, if required by the committee, provide a respectable householder as surety for the remainder of his payments.

7) Any member wishing to have articles of a greater value than the amount of his share, can do so by paying the difference at the time he takes the articles.

8) Any member paying up the value of his share can have the articles as soon as he has done so without waiting till the next draw.

9) Any member in arrear with his subscription or fines shall not be entitled to take part in the drawing of his share.

10) If any member leaving the town, or from illness, desires to withdraw his money, the same may be returned to him less a deduction of one penny in the shilling, but the committee shall have discretionary powers.

11) Every article supplied in the shop is marked in plain figures, off which Mr Fattorini will take a FIXED DISCOUNT to the club except silver spoons.

'Meetings with friends in public houses and the added attraction of a free supper did much to free this form of credit purchasing of the socially undesirable image of debt, when compared with other forms—eg, tally-men and pawnbrokers. The purchasing power of the working classes was at once extended, giving them the chance to purchase sound and desirable goods'.[1]

Indeed, it may be a surprise to those who believe in the utter poverty and deprivation of the Victorian working class to read through the list of goods available to members of the Fattorini purchasing clubs.

Gold watches	from £8
Silver watches	from £1. 1s
Gold Albert chains	from £1. 10s
Clocks of all kinds	from 8s. 6d
Wedding rings	from 7s. 6d
Cruet frames	from 8s. 0d
Knives and forks (half-dozen)	from 3s. 6d
Britannia metal tea pots	from 2s. 0d
Britannia metal coffee pots	from 5s. 0d
Tea spoons (half-dozen)	from 1s. 6d
Table spoons (half-dozen)	from 5s. 6d
Dessert spoons (half-dozen)	from 3s. 6d
Ladies' bags	from 3s. 6d
Ladies' work boxes	from 3s. 6d
Writing desks	from 3s. 6d
Hair brushes and combs of all kinds	
Jet goods of every description	
Sewing machines of any make	

[1]*The Fattorini Family and its Contribution to Mail Order Trading in the United Kingdom* (thesis by Valerie F. Dyson, Bradford, 1977).

RIGHT **The Fattorini Clubs started in the 1850s to supply watches to working men. By the 1890s they had become 'Watch, Clock & Jewellery Clubs' selling a variety of goods, including musical instruments. This was the beginning of the Fattorini mail order business.**

The habit of buying through purchasing clubs spread rapidly and the clubs soon formed a major part of the firm's business. By the turn of the century there were some 1,000 Fattorini clubs spread all over the country, and each one was in effect a small Fattorini branch that had a steady turnover without the expense of staff or premises. The success and spread of these 'branches' was due mainly to the continuation of the policy of good quality merchandise at lowest prices. Much effort too was put into what would today be called 'quality control'. This was particularly so in the case of watches which, in order to ensure absolute reliability, were ordered in quantities far in excess of actual requirements so that each batch could be kept going for some weeks under careful observation in the Kirkgate shop. Only those that kept near-perfect time were sold to the firm's customers, the rest were returned to the manufacturers. This practice of holding large stocks of watches led to the firm suffering a serious loss in February 1858 when thieves broke into the Bradford shop on a Sunday morning when the Fattorinis and their staff were at church. A great quantity of watches was taken together with other valuables, and although the burglars did not succeed in opening the safe their total haul was in the region of £1,800, a sum considered so large in those days that the newspapers referred to the incident as 'The Great Jewellery Robbery'.

Expansion

In March 1859 Antonio Fattorini died at the comparatively early age of 63. A man of great creative ability and independent thought, he had so built up his small business in both range and scope that at the time of his death his was a household name in the West Riding. On his death the firm broke into three separate parts although, to keep the name Fattorini well in the public eye, they continued to advertise jointly. This was done by printing one catalogue to be shared by the three firms, each adding its own distinctive front cover. Edward and John assumed joint proprietorship of the Bradford business, and Innocent at Skipton consolidated his independent position by initiating various business ventures of his own. The Harrogate business was inherited by the younger Antonio and it continued to prosper. Antonio never married and he let it be known to his brothers that he intended to

RIGHT **Antonio Fattorini in later life**

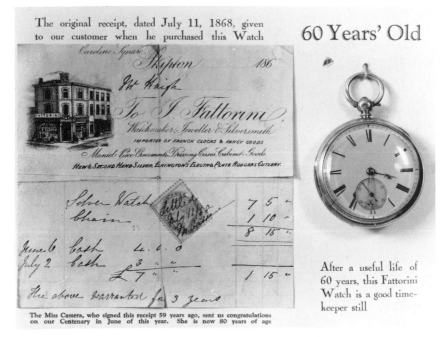

The original receipt, dated July 11, 1868, given to our customer when he purchased this Watch

60 Years' Old

After a useful life of 60 years, this Fattorini Watch is a good time-keeper still

The Miss Cassera, who signed this receipt 59 years ago, sent us congratulations on our Centenary in June of this year. She is now 80 years of age

A receipt for a Fattorini solid silver watch and chain for £8. 15s

RIGHT **Barometers and optical goods. Fattorini supplied spectacles from 1s. 0d per pair, sight test included. These spectacles were not made up but drawn from stock**

leave the business to his manager. Upon learning this, Edward and John persuaded him to have his sister, Marie Tindall, and her husband to look after him and this was agreed. In the event, the Tindalls inherited the business and it remains in Tindall hands today.

At the time of the elder Antonio's death the Bradford business had far outgrown the Kirkgate shop and additional space was required to allow for further expansion. In 1861 another large shop was opened in Bradford, this time at 28 Westgate, one of the town's busiest shopping streets. It appears that part of this building was already lived in by Edward and his family, for three years before the shop was opened he is recorded on the voting list to be at that address. The immediate advantages of opening in Westgate were twofold. In the first place the virtual doubling of shop space

BAROMETERS AND THERMOMETERS.

FITZROY BAROMETERS, warranted corrected, 16s.

FITZROY BAROMETERS in beautifully carved Oak and Walnut Cases, suitable for Halls and Passages, 35s. to 50s.

WHEEL BAROMETERS, from 18s. each, warranted correct

ANEROID BAROMETERS (without quicksilver), small, for the pocket, £2 10s.

Ditto, large, in Brass cases, 4 inches diameter, £1 7s.

Ditto, largest, 10 inches diameter, £2 10s.

THERMOMETERS in Box-wood, for Rooms, Baths, &c., 1s., 1s. 6d., and 2s.

THERMOMETERS for Brewers, in Metal cases, from 2s. 6d.

THERMOMETERS for out of doors to Register the extremes of heat and cold, 4s.

OPERA AND FIELD GLASSES,
OF ALL KINDS,
VERY POWERFUL,
From 10s. *to* 50s.

TELESCOPES, achromatic and non-achromatic, from 7s. 6d. to £5.

The higher priced ones are fitted with night-glasses for observing the moon and stars.

SPECTACLES.

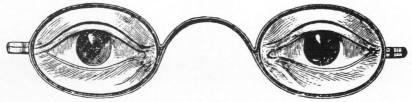

THE SIGHT ACCURATELY SUITED IN A FEW MINUTES WITHOUT ANY TROUBLE.

Spectacles to suit all sights from One Shilling the pair.

Spectacles with fine steel frames, 2s. 6d. the pair.

Spectacles with real Brazillian pebbles, 6s. 6d. and 7s. 6d.

Spectacles with coloured glasses, from 2s. 6d.

Concave Spectacles for near sights, from 2s. 6d.

Spectacles with solid gold frames, 18s.

Eye-glasses, in horn frames, 1s. 6d. the pair.

Eye-glasses, in solid gold, 15s. to 48s.

SEVERAL HUNDRED PAIRS to select from.

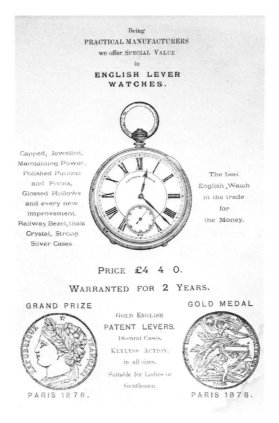

Being
PRACTICAL MANUFACTURERS
we offer SPECIAL VALUE
in
ENGLISH LEVER
WATCHES.

Capped, Jewelled,
Maintaining Power,
Polished Pinions
and Pivots,
Glossed Hollows
and every new
improvement.
Railway Bezel, thick
Crystal, Strong
Silver Cases

The best
English Watch
in the trade
for
the Money.

PRICE £4 4 0.

WARRANTED FOR 2 YEARS.

GRAND PRIZE

GOLD ENGLISH
PATENT LEVERS,
18-carat Cases.
KEYLESS ACTION.
in all sizes.
Suitable for Ladies or
Gentlemen.

GOLD MEDAL

PARIS 1878.

PARIS 1878.

A page from the 1879 catalogue. These were shared by all Fattorini
shops, each one having its own distinctive cover

enabled the firm greatly to enlarge its range of goods; secondly, it
allowed the Kirkgate shop to specialise in the better quality jewellery, plate and other luxury goods for which it was already
famous, while the Westgate branch concentrated on building up a
trade at the lower end of the market. In consequence of this
widening of range the catalogue was much enlarged and was
circulated not only to purchasing clubs but to the general public
and even found its way into the homes of the local gentry. It listed
'. . . watches from £1 to £250. Marble Clocks, the largest stock in
England' and, 'Barometers, Opera and Field Glasses, Pianos,
Harmoniums, American Organs, Sewing and Wringing Machines,
etc'. The clocks ranged from 'The Working Man's Clock' priced at

Bradford catalogue 1889

5s. od to a fine long-case (grandfather) chiming clock at £8. The better clocks and watches were 'warranted for five years—unless it gets broken'. Westgate started an optician's department that supplied 'spectacles to suit all sights from One Shilling'. This price included a sight test. Sometime during the 1870s the firm acquired machinery to manufacture its own watches and by 1887 was producing them in considerable numbers. At the Golden Jubilee Industrial Exhibition held at Saltaire, Yorkshire, in that year, Fattorini & Sons was commended not only on the extensive range of its watches but on the machinery for making them which the firm also exhibited. At that time Fattorinis were selling a great number of their watches to railwaymen who, by the conditions of their employment, were required to possess a timepiece. Advertising in the *Monthly Journal of the Society of Locomotive Engineers and Firemen*, a journal published for the 'social, moral and intellectual advancement of its members', Fattorini & Sons claimed that their 'three guinea lever watches are now in use by Engine Drivers and Guards on almost all the railways in the United Kingdom, and are guaranteed to stand both the jolting of the engine and the van'.

At this time the firm was doing a thriving business in regalia, trophies, medals and related goods. These were designed in Bradford by the company's own artists and executed by outside craftsmen in Birmingham. Fattorinis designed and supplied many pieces to commemorate famous events, provided gold and silver medals to schools and colleges, cups and medals to sporting clubs, awards for flower shows, chess clubs, learned societies and hundreds of other organisations throughout the country. They supplied mayoral chains, civic and masonic regalia, badges, caskets, centrepieces and various other ceremonial items. The firm also designed and supplied gaming counters and tradesmen's credit tokens, all bearing the name 'Fattorini'. One, a gaming token with a figure of a man playing cards, gives the maker as 'Fattorini of Skipton, Harrogate and Bradford', thus showing that the three shops still followed a policy of jointly promoting the family name. By the turn of the century the trophy, medal and token work had become an important part of the three businesses.

The trade in sporting trophies was greatly increased following the arrival in Bradford in 1882 of another Antonio Fattorini, who became well known all over the district and beyond as a keen and accomplished sportsman. Born in 1862, this Antonio was a nephew of the Bradford brothers and a grandson of the founder of the business. His father, Frank, was a gentleman farmer in Cumberland. After spending part of his early life with his bachelor namesake in Harrogate (where he learned watchmaking), this Antonio married and settled near Bradford. Because of his knowledge of watches he became known all over Britain as a sporting timekeeper, eventually acting in this capacity at the Olympic Games. Although he never joined the Bradford firm in an executive capacity, his sporting interests had a considerable effect upon it for, by recommendation, he helped his uncles, John and Edward, to build up an extensive trade in trophies for the sporting world. All these goods were made to the firm's own designs by sub-contractors in Birmingham and were traded through the Kirkgate shop.

The start of mail order

In 1890 the Kirkgate shop and its neighbours were demolished to make way for the new Midland railway station and its adjoining Midland Hotel. The business was moved to a bigger shop (also on a corner) where the range of good-quality merchandise was enlarged. At about the same time the Westgate shop extended its trade into a general range of household goods: blankets, sheets and other household linen, linoleum, rugs and mats. These formed the basis for the firm's first proper mail order catalogue, a catalogue, that is, not primarily aimed at selling jewellery, watches and plate but one which offered many of the everyday requirements that people would normally have obtained in a shop; and the customer was given an assurance that 'orders and enquiries will be as intelligently dealt with as though purchased over the counter'. In the years to follow the mail order department greatly extended its trade by offering clothing, footwear, materials for dressmaking and (for Sunday best) cheap furs and paletots. Later, bedsteads and other articles of furniture could be found in the catalogue together with bicycles and pianos. Everything was for immediate delivery and obtainable on 'weekly terms'. One of the best-selling items at that time was Fattorini's 'working man's eight-day alarm clock', which sold at £1. 5s. 'Send five shillings today,' said the catalogue, 'and the clock will be dispatched to you tomorrow.' This promise was not only a credit to the firm's customer service but expressed absolute confidence in the efficiency of the Victorian post office.

By 1907 the mail order side of the business had grown so large that it was decided to detach it from the retail shops and set up a separate company to deal with it. This, the eventual parent of Empire Stores, was the Northern Trading Company which was established in a large warehouse at 20 Sackville Street, Bradford. Recalling the starting of Northern Trading and the extraordinary pace of its early growth, one employee (then a young boy) recorded:

> First load to come was boots and shoes, one floor above ground. Then gents' clothes, then bicycles—50, all types, then carpets, rugs and lino. In 12 months, furniture. Then adverts were put in all the papers, 'Agents Wanted', and in no time the staff in the office was increased from 6 to 14 and up and up. Bicycles were our best sellers, and if we ran short I was given the job of going to Dysons in Park Road to collect different cycles I could ride. Empire Stores (sic) grew out of all expectations and all of a sudden Bradford was full of agents. Everywhere you went, mills and workrooms had one.

Northern Trading agents were not only active in Bradford but all over the north of England, for in addition to advertising the firm had representatives to recruit new agents at pitheads, public houses and factory gates. In those days a husband was responsible for his wife's debts and the firm only accepted men as agents, although in practice it was usually the wives who did the work. These agents acted as salesmen to their friends, neighbours and workmates, delivered the goods and collected the weekly payments through a system of open, continuous credit. For this they received a commission.

Potential mail order customers at the turn of the century
By courtesy of the GLC Library

Open credit

Through its club business the firm had dealt with the more prosperous sections of the working classes, those who could afford to buy silver watches and chains and other luxuries, albeit on the instalment plan. But by offering a comprehensive range of household goods and clothing on an open credit system, Northern Trading was appealing to an entirely different kind of customer: to large families managing to exist on £1. 10s or less a week, people to whom blankets were a luxury, sheets unknown and whose children were often forced to go barefoot. A typical week's budget of such a family was recorded by the social worker Maud Pember Reeves in her book *Round About a Pound a Week*.[1] The family consisted of a man, his wife and six children, and the total income was £1. 4s a week, of which the husband kept two shillings for spending money. The rest was spent by the wife as follows:

	s	d
Rent	5	0
Burial insurance[2]	2	0
Half cwt coal		8
Wood		1
Gas		3
Soap, soda		$4\frac{1}{2}$
Lamp oil		2
Matches		1
Husband's bus fares	1	0
Newspaper		2
Children's Band of Hope		3
Mending boots (at home)	1	0
Material for dress		6
Pair of stockings		$4\frac{1}{2}$
Boy's coat (made at home)		9
	12	8

Left for food for eight people, 9s. 4d. which was spent thus: 14 loaves, 2s. 11d; meat, 2s. 9d; 3lb sugar, 6d; butter, 10d; tea, 8d; 17lb potatoes, 9d; 1 tin milk, 3d; pot herbs and greens, 4d; 1lb jam, 4d.

[1] *Virago edition* (London, 1979), p. 87.

[2] *The weekly payment for burial insurance was one of the most important items in a poor family's budget at this time for the ultimate disgrace was for any member to be buried 'on the parish.' For a family of eight the cost of burial insurance was high.*

John Fattorini who led the
company into mail order

As there was no extra money at any time of the year clothes had
to be bought or made as they were required, and paid for as they
(or the material) was bought. Often this meant spending even less
on food or going without such necessities as coal, oil or soap. But
through the system of continuous credit Northern Trading made it
possible for the impoverished to attain a standard of living which,
however humble, was otherwise beyond their reach. Women
bringing up large families on about a pound a week were used to
having a definite weekly expenditure which hardly ever varied.
They needed to know how they stood; they tended to buy the same
items of food week by week so that they could calculate to a nicety
exactly how the money would last. To be able to buy clothes in the
same way held a great attraction for them. To such, the 'weekly'

system was ideal, and if the supplier of the goods, in addition to accepting small regular payments, sent an agent to collect the amount, the convenience of the transaction left nothing to be desired. From the company's point of view the key to success lay in careful buying. The goods had to be strong and durable enough to wear at least until paid for (and the period was sometimes longer than 20 weeks), and at the same time they had to be of the cheapest quality if they were to appeal to people whose average income was £1. 10s a week. Here it was essential for the Fattorinis to keep to their policy of low profits, high turnover, and value for money.

Sports & Pastimes

During the same year that Northern Trading Company was established, 1907, another separate concern was started by Fattorinis. This was the retail firm of Sports & Pastimes, set up to take advantage of the Kirkgate shop's ever-growing trade in sports trophies by selling sporting clothes and equipment as well, goods that would have been out of place in a jeweller's shop. Like all Fattorini ventures Sports & Pastimes was started to supply a definite social need, for the opening of the shop occurred at a time when there was a significant expansion in what is now called the leisure industry. People were working shorter hours and taking longer and more frequent holidays; they were spending more time and money on leisure, and local authorities and industry were providing more recreational facilities in the form of playing fields, swimming pools and the like. The new venture occupied a large shop in Bradford's Cheapside and was advertised as being 'a firm in the famous Fattorini & Sons Limited Group'. Sports & Pastimes was a success and, apart from the business done in the shop, was soon supplying sports organisations, schools and colleges all over the country.

An important event in 1911 that further enhanced the company's reputation in sporting circles was the winning by the Kirkgate establishment of a competition to design and supply a new silver cup for the Football Association. The entries were judged by a selection committee that included some of the most renowned silversmiths in the country and the Fattorini design was chosen from 250 other entries. The cup, 19 inches high and weighing 175 ounces, is the one played for at Wembley today. It cost 50 guineas (£52.50). By a happy coincidence Bradford won the cup that year by beating Newcastle United in a replay at Manchester.

Bradford City team in 1911 after winning the Football Association Cup designed and supplied by Fattorinis that year
By courtesy of The Telegraph and Argus, Bradford

End of an era

In 1909 John Fattorini died aged 77. Born in the year following the establishment of the original shop in Leeds market he lived to see the business grow and diversify into an important, complex organisation. It was he who pioneered the early club trading and developed it into a mail order business. The historian E. J. Hobsbawn writes:[1]

> The somnolence of the economy was already obvious in British society in the last decades before 1914. Already the rare dynamic entrepreneurs of Edwardian Britain were, more often than not, foreigners or members of minority groups . . . who understood . . . the massive social changes which provided a new opportunity for distributors.

That, in a phrase, describes the life and work of John Fattorini.

[1]*Industry and Empire* (London, 1963).

Parcel delivery c1908
Post Office copyright reserved

In December of the same year a private limited company was formed to take over the whole of the Bradford business and its subsidiaries. This company, Fattorini & Sons Limited, had a nominal share capital of £100,000 and all the shares were held by members of the family. Edward John Fattorini became chairman of a board of directors which consisted of Edward Joseph, Herbert Piero, Leo Francis and Tony Fattorini.

PART 2

Empire Stores
1910–1980

A new name—and a quarrel

In 1910 it was decided to separate the mail order business from the firm's other activities, and an application was made to the Registrar of Companies to incorporate Northern Trading Stores as a limited company in its own right. The application was refused by the Registrar on the grounds that another firm was already registered in that name, and it was the Registrar himself who suggested that the new name should be Empire Stores Limited. This was agreed and the company was registered on 28th June 1910 with a nominal share capital of £100. As in the case of the parent company all the shares were taken up by members of the Fattorini family.

Within two years of the establishment of Empire Stores there was a serious crisis in its affairs when John Enrico Fattorini, son of the chairman, Edward John Fattorini, quarrelled with his cousin Herbert who was then running the mail order side of the business. As a result Enrico resigned as mail order marketing manager and went off to start his own jewellery and mail order business in Manchester Road, Bradford. The main cause of the break was that Enrico was a strong individualist who disliked taking orders and despised business meetings where, in his opinion, more heat was generated than light. He was a natural entrepreneur with strong intuitions in business matters and he liked to make quick decisions. In the event his decision to break away on his own was, for him, the right one. At first he overtraded, a fatal mistake in the mail order

LEFT **The Kirkgate shop, Bradford, at the turn of the century**

53

Empire Stores' first warehouse and offices, Sackville Street, Bradford

industry, and had to turn to his father for financial backing, but he learned from his mistake and never repeated it. Soon he had the business on a sound footing. Other Fattorinis had in the past broken away from the Bradford firm to become independent but all had continued in a spirit of co-operation with the others. Enrico was the first (and only) member of the family to set up in direct rivalry with the rest. At first he traded under the name of John E. Fattorini, much to the annoyance of the directors of the original firm who alleged that he was unfairly trading on the good reputation of his uncle John Edward Fattorini, then a Bradford JP and well known in the town for his civic interests. Enrico, in fairness, countered this accusation by stating in his catalogues, 'I have no connection with any other firm trading under a similar name'. But even this did not satisfy the rest of the family and they took the matter to court. There it was held that no man can be prevented from trading under his own name. However, having won the fight, Enrico dropped the use of his name and renamed his firm Grattan Warehouses Limited, after the street from which he was then operating. In competition with the Fattorini mail order business, Enrico's venture flourished to become one of the biggest firms of its kind in the country.

Quick deliveries

During the first year of trading as an independent concern Empire Stores made a net profit of £10,417, a result which the directors found highly satisfactory. It had been achieved in competition with the high street shops which were at the time engaged in a fierce price war among themselves. In addition, the larger shops and chain stores, such as Samuels and Ludlows, were all offering 'easy payments'. The West Riding Furnishing Company was advertising 'Gradual Payment System From the Shop' as were Morrisons of Birmingham and many other famous shops. The Co-operative Societies, too, with their cut prices and dividends, were growing in popularity. Empire Stores competed successfully with these rivals by rigorously applying the low profit policy and maintaining a system of fast delivery which often put goods into customers' hands on the day following receipt of an order. This was achieved no matter where the customer lived, for the company could rely absolutely on the efficiency of the post office for parcels, and on the railways for delivery of bulkier goods. Local and district parcel deliveries were undertaken by the Bradford tramways system which then had lines running as far as Leeds (passenger fare 4d return). The parcels were collected by the tram company and taken to a central depot from whence they were carried by tram to various sub-depots. There they were taken over by the tram company's own messenger boys[1] who delivered them to the customers' doors. The charge for this service, irrespective of distance, was 3d for parcels up to 14lb and 5d for those up to 28lb. To Empire Stores the great advantage of this service was that it enabled goods to be delivered to local customers on the same day their orders were received.

[1] *It is an interesting point that the Italian word 'fattorini' means 'messengers or deliverers of goods'.*

Trams in Sunbridge Road, Bradford
Copyright Walter Scott, Bradford

Following the first three successful years it was decided to form a subsidiary company to act as a buying agent for Empire Stores, for it was realised that a separate wholesale firm would obtain better business terms than those normally available to a retail house. The new firm was named (for want of a better idea) E. Robertshaw & Company Limited after the parent company's then secretary, E. Robertshaw. Starting as a wholesaler for radios and gramophones the business grew until it was supplying not only Empire Stores' requirements in this field but many retailers in and around Bradford. Later Robertshaws won many large and important contracts with hospital boards, municipal authorities and similar bodies for the supply of linen, industrial clothing and domestic goods.

FATTORINI & SONS, LTD., WESTGATE, BRADFORD.

WESTGATE ESTABLISHMENT.

We are actual manufacturers and our customers have the assurance that a
house which has enjoyed the public confidence for nearly a
century is at the back of every article purchased.

ABOVE & OVERLEAF **Illustrations from a Fattorini brochure of 1915**

57

KIRKGATE ESTABLISHMENT.

This illustration shows our present place of business. We purchased this building from the executors of the late Mr. Wm. Byles, in which the "*Bradford Observer*" was printed for many years.

The three floors over our present shop cover an area of nearly 6,000 square feet. The rooms are occupied by Watch and Clockmakers, Jewellers, Polishers etc The remainder of the space is used exclusively by the staff engaged in our medal, badge, cup, etc. department and our mail-order and foreign trade The whole of the staff, along with one of the Managing Directors. devote their whole attention to this section of our business, which has ramifications all over the world wherever the English tongue is spoken

Sheriff's Chain
and
Badge of Office.

The City
of
London.

FATTORINI & SONS, LTD., WESTGATE, BRADFORD.

For latest styles in Ladies' Paletots, Costumes, Skirts, Blouses, etc., we beg to refer you to our up-to-date Drapery List published at frequent intervals and sent post free.

The excellent quality of the goods supplied by **Fattorini & Sons, Ltd.,** is common knowledge the world over, and a comparison of their prices affords further proof of the many advantages which purchasers enjoy in shopping by Mail with this old established and reliable House.

Empire Stores Ltd.—Corner Views of Drapery, Lino and Carpet Departments.

Customers' requirements are studied to the minutest detail ; all orders are executed with facility and despatch— the same careful and prompt attention being bestowed on small as on large orders.

We do an enormous trade with residents in all parts of the Globe and our splendid organisation for dealing prompt - ly and efficiently with all kinds of business has earned us the praise of thousands of purchasers.

Empire Stores, Ltd.—Corner Views, Furnishing Section

PROVINCIAL & DISTRICT GRAND OFFICERS' APRONS

Manufactured by

FATTORINI & SONS, LTD., BRADFORD

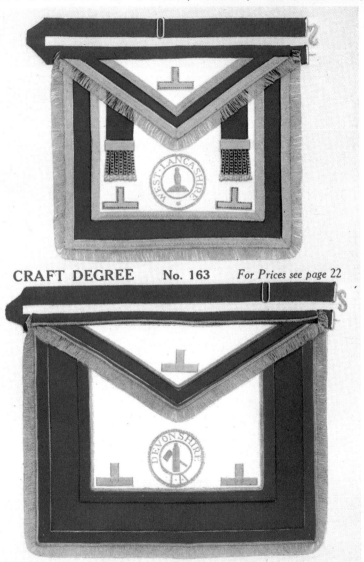

CRAFT DEGREE   No. 163   *For Prices see page 22*

The Great War

The years of the First World War made little difference to the business of Empire Stores and it continued to expand despite shortages of consumer goods. The other branches of the Fattorini group also grew during that period. In 1915 a company was formed to manufacture the large quantities of school and sports clothing then being handled by Sports & Pastimes. This was called Bradford Textile Limited and operated from a factory in Cheapside.

The war brought substantial government contracts to the Kirkgate shop for cap badges, shoulder titles and other insignia for Britain's new armies. The manufacture of most of these articles was by the famous and long-established Birmingham firm of Joseph Moore, which was then sub-contractor for most of the Bradford firm's special orders. By 1915 Fattorinis' trade in medals, and masonic, civil and military regalia had become a major part of the business and therefore an approach was made to the management of Joseph Moores with a view to merging the two firms. In the event, Fattorini & Sons purchased the Birmingham firm outright for £3,133. 8s. 7d.

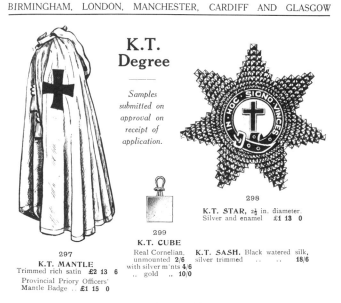

BIRMINGHAM, LONDON, MANCHESTER, CARDIFF AND GLASGOW

K.T. Degree

Samples submitted on approval on receipt of application.

297
K.T. MANTLE
Trimmed rich satin **£2 13 6**
Provincial Priory Officers'
Mantle Badge .. **£1 15 0**

299
K.T. CUBE
Real Cornelian,
unmounted **2/6**
with silver m'nts **4/6**
.. gold .. **10/0**

K.T. SASH. Black watered silk,
silver trimmed **18/6**

298
K.T. STAR, 2½ in. diameter.
Silver and enamel **£1 13 0**

LEFT, ABOVE & OVERLEAF **Masonic regalia made by Fattorinis 1921**

PROVINCIAL & DISTRICT GRAND OFFICERS' JEWELS

Manufactured by

FATTORINI & SONS, LTD., BRADFORD

**ROYAL
ARCH
DEGREE**

*For Prices
see
page 42*

No. 228

MARK DEGREE

No. 278

CRAFT DEGREE

No. 168

Joseph Moores

The original Joseph Moore, founder of the Birmingham firm, was one of Britain's greatest medallists. Born at Eastbourne in 1817, he began an apprenticeship with a firm of silversmiths at the age of 10. There he became expert at drawing, medal designing and die sinking. Later he started his own business as a maker of dies for button manufacture, when that was Birmingham's biggest industry. He then established himself as a medallist and, while still a young man, became known all over the world for the fine quality of his work. In 1844 Moore went into partnership with another well known medallist, John Allen, but that venture failed in 1856. He then started again on his own account in Summer Lane, Birmingham, moving shortly afterwards to Pitsford Street where he worked until his death in 1892. Moore's place was taken by his son Joseph, who was also a noted medallist. He built up the firm considerably, concentrating largely on medals and masonic regalia. At Joseph's death the business was taken over by his sons Joseph and Frank, and it was they who negotiated with Fattorinis. Trading as the Birmingham branch of Fattorini & Sons the firm continued to progress. Its period of war work finished in 1919 with the making of hundreds of gold and silver peace medals for towns and villages all over the country and a million similar medals in base metal.

Hard times

In 1918 the Fattorini group profit was £15,593 of which £9,330 was contributed by Empire Stores. Throughout the war the company's catalogue had hardly altered in format or content: even prices had hardly changed despite wartime inflation. A three-piece solid oak bedroom suite could be bought for £10, a good quality bicycle for £7. 7s, a chiming mantel clock for £1. 2s (2s. 0d down and 10 payments of 2s. 0d). Boots were 10s. 0d a pair, and the range of watches started at 6s. 6d. 'We will never be satisfied until our customers are,' said the catalogue, on which was displayed the outline drawing of a box, or parcel, which had become the firm's emblem.

The post-war boom in Britain was short lived and followed by the sequence of economic crises and depressions with which the 1920s and 1930s were beset. Times were bad for the retail trade in general but for Empire Stores they were years of growth. In 1920 occurred the first crisis, and over the following two years the prices of goods fell sharply. This was the result of a deliberate policy of deflation by the government, which drew the then vast sum of £70 million from the economy, thus considerably changing the ratio between currency and production. The result was that many manufacturers, although continuing to expand output, began employing techniques and methods of cost reduction which increased output at lower cost. As a consequence wages fell drastically during 1921-22 and unemployment increased.

> The Ministry of Labour recorded an average decrease in 1921 of 17s. 6d a week for 7.2 million workers, and a further 11s. 0d in 1922 for 7.6 million: coal miners did much worse than this, losing an average £2 a week in 1921 and another 10s. 0d the next year.[1]

It is a fact that in those days the mail order industry tended to prosper in hard times, for the newly unemployed were forced to resort to the 'weekly' to obtain many necessities such as clothes, bedding and other domestic items. In the 1920s and 1930s mail order demand rose to record heights, for the period was characterised by unemployment: the north of England, where mail order had always been popular, was particularly badly hit. Between 1921 and 1938 it was estimated that on average one in every 10 working people was out of a job, and in seven of those years at least three out of 20 were unemployed. In absolute figures unemployment ranged from a minimum of just over a million to a maximum (in 1932) of nearly three million. On the other hand, the standard of living for those in employment actually rose during the years 1923-38: this was because wages during that period remained relatively stable while the cost of food fell, making extra money available to be spent on clothing, domestic appliances and furnishings.

As Empire Stores continued to grow, its army of agents and its catalogues increased in size year by year. By 1929 the Sackville Street warehouse was outgrown and a move was made to the much larger building in Canal Road that is now the company's head office. With more space available a new countrywide drive to recruit agents was initiated, and by 1930 over 8,000 were receiving the catalogue. Agents then received 15 per cent commission on paid-up accounts and 20 per cent for cash sales. As today, all

[1]*Burnett, John. A History of the Cost of Living* (Harmondsworth, 1969).

Unemployment queue 1924
BBC Hulton Picture Library

postage charges (including poundage on postal orders) was paid by
the company. Empire Stores also took responsibility for bad debts,
although it warned the new agent to be 'very cautious as to the
amount of business he accepts in one house or in one family, and
keep first orders small until experience is gained'. At six per cent,
bad debts were surprisingly low when the prevailing shortage of
money is considered.

The mechanics and administration of the business seem
remarkably simple compared with those of today. Every order that
came to Canal Road was scrutinised by a director and, if approved,
marked 'SEND'. A girl then took a basket from department to
department and assembled the order; stock control and ledger
entries were made by pen and ink, the invoices were typed and the
order dispatched.

The 'thirties catalogues

Empire Stores' catalogues at this time were published in a number of separate parts, one for clothing, another for furniture, others for footwear, drapery, leather goods, jewellery, cutlery, watches, etc. To browse through them is to study both the realities of present-day inflation and the far-reaching changes in social life that have occurred during the last 50 years or so.

There are ladies' dresses ranging from a fully flared model with belt, buckles and buttons for 2s. 6d to a taffeta evening dress (£1. 9s. 11d). There is a 'splendid outfit for housemaids in poplin, with collar, cuffs and apron' (13s. 6d). At the other end of the scale are

F **1864**

1929

Atlas Novaphonic Portable Model.

CASE · ·	Leatherette Covered with strong corners and lock. Strong handle, Nickel-plated Combined Needle Cups and Record Cleaner.
SIZE · · ·	16½in. x 12in. x 7in.
MOTOR ·	Single Spring Garrard.
TURN-TABLE	10in. Plush Covered Turntable. Dial Speed Indicator.
SOUND BOX	Metal Diaphram Sound Box.
TONE ARM	Bugle shaped and Metal Amplifier designed to give maximum tone and volume.
RECORD CARRIER	Fitted in lid in design as shewn.

Price   **£4 : 10 : 0**

1930

J 2277

Stylish Silver Wristlet Watch for Gent's wear,
with Leather Strap. 15 Jewel Lever Movement.
Assorted shapes and dials.

Price - **£2/5/-**

squirrel fur ties (£1. 3s. 6d) or squirrel wraps (£6. 5s). Demurely
illustrated feminine underwear includes corsets (5s. 0d to 15s. 0d),
'smart combinations' (4s. 0d to 12s. 0d a pair) and 'dainty garters'
at 1s. 6d. For men there are two-piece suits at £1. 19s. 6d ready
made or, at £5. 15s, made to measure (the agent did the measur-
ing). The prices of jewellery and optical goods seemed hardly to
have changed in the firm's century of trading: rolled-gold Albert
watch chains at 12s. 6d, watch seals and rings from 6s. 6d,
barometers at 18s. 0d and binoculars from 16s. 0d a pair. The £1
watch was still on offer in 1931, although no longer in a silver case.
In the toy catalogue can be found many tinplate items priced at a

Our Speed Kings' Models in Miniature.

SILVER BULLET. MECHANICAL RACING MOTOR.

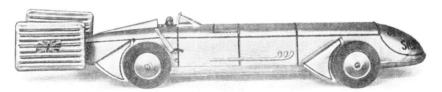

F 2212

A wonderful reproduction of Kaye Don's Silver Bullet. Beautifully constructed, every part
representing the original as near as possible. Even the speed will astound you, the spring being
specially made and very quick in action. A Mechanical Model that will please every boy.

1930   Length approx. 22½ ins.   Price **8/11** each.

1931

M 593

Tasteful **Collar** and **Cuff Set** in fine quality **Beaverette**. High collar thats fits well up and the very latest shaped cuffs.   This set will greatly add to the appearance of your ensemble. Ready for immediate attachment.

Price · **27/6** the Set.

M 592

Magnificent **Collar** and **Cuff Set** of **Finest Nutria Lamb**. The extra broad cuffs fit right up to the elbow in latest point style. A real heavy quality set that will greatly add to the value of any coat. Is ready for immediate attachment.

Price - **45/6** the Set.

Fur Trimming for

Ladies' Coats.

M 594

Luxurious is this **Collar** and **Cuff Set** in rich **Sablette**.   Easily attached to any coat with pleasing results.   The fur is tastefully marked and possesses a fascinating sheen. The very thing to smarten up your coat.   Good value at a moderate price.

Price - **17/6** the Set.

few shillings which now fetch many pounds in the sale rooms, a striking example being a model of a famous racing car priced at 7s. 0d, one of which recently fetched £220 at a Christies' auction sale. For years the toy catalogue had been advertising indoor games as 'pleasing for winter evenings', but during the 1920s and 1930s, dull evenings in millions of British homes were transformed through the purchase of gramophones and later wireless sets. Empire Stores first began dealing in gramophones with the issue of a catalogue of machines ranging in price from £2. 10s ('complete with gramophone records') to a 'console model in Jacobean style' at £6. 10s ('complete with six records of twelve popular tunes'). Radios appeared in about 1930. 'How much a year do you spend on the pictures?' asked an Empire Stores' advertisement. 'How much a

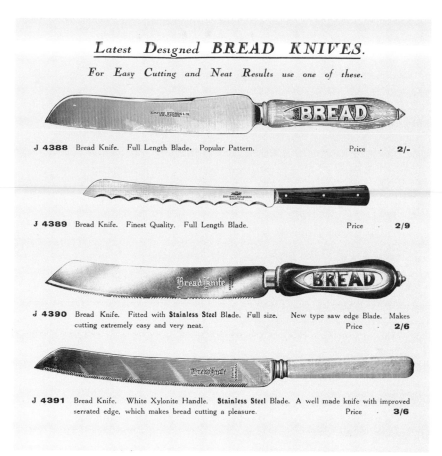

Latest Designed BREAD KNIVES.

For Easy Cutting and Neat Results use one of these.

J 4388 Bread Knife. Full Length Blade. Popular Pattern. Price . **2/-**

J 4389 Bread Knife. Finest Quality. Full Length Blade. Price . **2/9**

J 4390 Bread Knife. Fitted with **Stainless Steel** Blade. Full size. New type saw edge Blade. Makes cutting extremely easy and very neat. Price . **2/6**

J 4391 Bread Knife. White Xylonite Handle. **Stainless Steel** Blade. A well made knife with improved serrated edge, which makes bread cutting a pleasure. Price . **3/6**

1932

year do you spend on theatres? How much a year do you spend on reading materials? How much a year does your pleasure cost you? HOW MUCH A YEAR WOULD IT COST YOU TO GET YOUR PLEASURE FROM A GOOD RADIO?—A LOT LESS!' Then follows a list of 160 radio stations with their wavelengths. Those early sets ranged in price from £8 to £93 (the latter figure being equivalent to a year's wages for some people) for a 'radio-gramophone in a mahogany case'. For the 'do it yourself' enthusiast there was a radio assembly kit for £7.

Those who preferred their music 'live' were invited by Empire Stores to 'LEARN TO PLAY ONE OF OUR FAMOUS MUSICAL INSTRUMENTS AND BE THE LIFE AND SOUL OF THE PARTY'. The 'famous instruments' were the piano-accordion at £2. 18s. 6d, the concertina (£1. 7s. 6d), the banjo (£1. 12s. 6d), the ukulele (5s. 6d) and the banjulele (6s. 6d). There were no television sets in the catalogues of those times, but in 1936 there was a mains-driven 9.5 mm film projector for 19s. 6d; the screen and its stand cost an extra 3s. 6d.

It is hard to grasp today that a lady's dress could be bought for what it now costs to post a letter, or that binoculars could be obtained for today's price of a couple of loaves of bread, but it must be kept in mind that in those days a three-bedroomed house could be built for £500, that a new car could cost no more than £100, that petrol was 2s. 0d a gallon, gin 11s. 0d a bottle, train travel 1d a mile, and that a housemaid could be employed for £75 a year.

One hundred years

Although the company grew throughout the years of depression it suffered its own troubles as the economic situation worsened in the 1930s. The general and prolonged shortage of money forced many manufacturers out of business with the not infrequent result that some items offered in the catalogue could not be supplied. The money shortage also caused a serious slow-down in payments of customers' accounts, and in 1933, when the slump was at its worst and money at its scarcest, the company was compelled to take its own economy measures. The crisis was dealt with by agreed salary cuts in top management, a stopping of staff recruitment, and a 'freeze' on all wages. In this way redundancies were avoided. Yet despite the seriousness of the situation it was then that Empire Stores started giving its staff a fortnight's paid holiday a year.

In the very depths of the depression the company celebrated its first 100 years with widespread festivities for its staff. It had evolved throughout a century of change in social and economic conditions, manufacturing techniques, retail distribution patterns and consumer demand; always expanding, but slowly and cautiously by careful adaptation to the ever-changing times.

Survival

The other branches of the business also managed to survive and even to expand during the difficult years of the 1920s and 1930s. In 1920 Bradford Textile, the group's clothing manufacturers, moved into larger premises at 11 and 13 Snowden Street. Here, 130 people

1932

M 1009

Most attractive is this Coat for Maids, cut from serviceable quality **Flecked Tweed.**
The semi-fitting single breasted fastening is essentially neat, and is finished with all-round belt. Complete with slip pockets and the fashionable stitched collar. Lined throughout. In **Emerald Green** or **Cherry Flecked Tweed.**

Lengths;

40in.　42in.　44in.

Price - **22/6**

M 1010

Fancy Barathea is the material from which this Maids and Ladies Coat has been produced. The back is tastefully designed as illustrated with strappings of self material reversed. Well styled revers terminate in single breasted fastening Two slip pockets. Lined throughout. Utmost satisfaction assured. In **Fancy Navy** or **Fancy Brown Barathea.**

MAIDS.

Lengths - 42in.　44in.

Price - **42/-**

LADIES.

Sizes - W　W　OS
Lengths 46in. 48in. 48in.

Price - **44/-**

M 1060

Expertly modelled Coat for Maids and Ladies in good quality **Wool Hopsack.** Cut with the new adaptable revers in double-breasted style. All round belt, slip pockets Choicely lined throughout. A superior model in **Almond Green** or **Brick Red,**

Lengths:

42in.　44in.　46in.

Price - **52/-**

M 1011

A stylish semi-fitting Coat in reliable quality **Barathea.** In double-breasted style is fitted two slip pockets and well defined revers. Two buttons finish each sleeve. Lined throughout. A charming model for Maids and Ladies. In **Navy** or **Dark Green.**

Sizes:

SW　W　W　OS

Lengths:

40in. 42in. 44in. 46in.

Prices:

46/6　**48/6**

were employed in a variety of activities which included the making of religious vestments, caps for international sportsmen and embroidered badges for sportswear. During the following year the Kirkgate shop, having been outgrown, was moved to bigger premises at 21 Kirkgate. In 1928 Sports & Pastimes also moved to more spacious premises, in Market Street, and 10 years later to 37 Westgate which was larger still.

The Birmingham business continued to grow as its products became sought after all over the world. By 1930 it had showrooms in London, Cardiff, Glasgow and Manchester. The firm's 1931 brochure illustrates 'presentation pieces for their Majesties King George and Queen Mary, their late Majesties King Edward and Queen Alexandra, his Majesty the King of Spain, etc'. By this time Birmingham was supplying masonic lodges not only with 'jewels and furniture' but with a full range of masonic clothing, aprons, collars, gauntlets, etc, most of which was made by Bradford Textile. The only serious setback suffered by the Birmingham branch during this period was through a fire that occurred at the factory in March 1937. It was fought by 70 firemen with 17 fire

1932

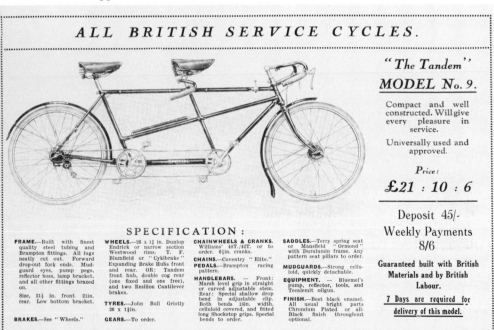

ALL BRITISH SERVICE CYCLES.

"The Tandem"

MODEL No. 9.

Compact and well constructed. Will give every pleasure in service.

Universally used and approved.

Price:

£21 : 10 : 6

Deposit 45/-
Weekly Payments
8/6

Guaranteed built with British Materials and by British Labour.

7 Days are required for delivery of this model.

SPECIFICATION :

FRAME.—Built with finest quality steel tubing and Brampton fittings. All lugs neatly cut out. Forward drop-out fork ends. Mudguard eyes, pump pegs, reflector boss, lamp bracket, and all other fittings brazed on.
Size, 21½ in. front. 21in. rear. Low bottom bracket.

BRAKES.—See "Wheels."

WHEELS.—26 x 1½ in. Dunlop Endrick or narrow section Westwood rims. T. F. Blumfield or "Cyklbrake" Expanding Brake Hubs front and rear. OR: Tandem front hub, double cog rear (one fixed and one free), and two Resilion Cantilever brakes.

TYRES.—John Bull Gristly 26 x 1⅜in.

GEARS.—To order.

CHAINWHEELS & CRANKS. Williams' 48T./42T. or to order. 6½in. cranks.

CHAINS.—Coventry "Elite."

PEDALS.—Brampton racing pattern.

HANDLEBARS. — Front: Marsh level grip in straight or curved adjustable stem. Rear: Special shallow drop bend in adjustable clip. Both bends 1½in. width, celluloid covered, and fitted long Shockstop grips. Special bends to order.

SADDLES.—Terry spring seat or Mansfield "Ormond" with Duralumin frame. Any pattern seat pillars to order.

MUDGUARDS.—Strong celluloid, quickly detachable.

EQUIPMENT. — Bluemel's pump, reflector, tools, and Tecalemit oilgun.

FINISH.—Best black enamel. All usual bright parts Chromium Plated or all-Black finish throughout optional.

engines. Fortunately no one was hurt, but there was a considerable loss of gold and silver goods.

There were signs of recovery from the depression all over Britain after 1935 and this recovery continued throughout the remainder of the decade.

In 1936 the business of Fattorini & Sons was under the general management of three Fattorini brothers, Edward and Leo (who jointly ran the jewellery business) and Herbert who managed Empire Stores. With the depressed years behind, the country's economy was buoyant and there was a feeling of optimism for the future in the air. In the Fattorini group all departments were still expanding. In 1937 the Kirkgate business moved again, this time into modern shop premises in Tyrell Street (where it is today). There the firm offered one year's free insurance on all items of jewellery purchased, a practice which led Edward Fattorini to ask sadly on more than one occasion, 'What do you do when you see a customer wearing a piece of jewellery on which you have paid out insurance two years ago?' The Tyrell Street shop also allowed jewellery to go out to known customers 'on approval' which, on

1932

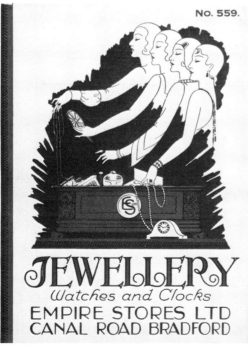

NO. 559.

JEWELLERY
Watches and Clocks
EMPIRE STORES LTD
CANAL ROAD BRADFORD

J 4498

Solid Silver, Hall-marked Gold Centre . . . **5/-**
9ct. Gold, Hall-marked - **22/-**

J 4545

18ct. Gold Five-Stone Diamond Ring with White Gold, Claw or Millgrain Setting.

Price - **£4/5/-**

Lovely Undies — A Delight to Wear

D 3151	D 3152	D 3153	D 3154	D 3029
Non - ladder **Art. Silk** of lovely texture makes this Skirt and Knicker Set, beautifully decorated with a Satin appliqued motif and edged with lace round the top. Front basque style Directoire Knickers trimmed to match.	Non - ladder **Art. Silk** with a Satiny sheen forms this Set which many will favour. Beautiful motif of lace, satin and coloured embroidery; elastic under arms, carefully cut top; Directoire knickers, trimmed by motif. You'll **feel** smart with this under your dress. As illustration and similar.	With a large Satin motif, embroidered in colours, this Ladies' Princess Slip and Knicker Set is in heavy non-ladder Art. Silk. It is also daintily embroidered in Art. Silk on the French lace - edged Knickers in which bulkiness is guarded against by a front basque.	Matron's Skirt and Knicker Set in lustrous **non - ladder Art. Silk.** Directoire Knickers with front basque and motif. Skirt has beautiful motif of lace and Art. Silk and elastic inserts under arms for snug fit.	A one-piece Ca⟨⟩ Knicker that is id⟨⟩ for wear under ⟨⟩ modern "slink⟨⟩" dresses for day ⟨⟩ evening wear. In ⟨⟩ latest style it is ⟨⟩ non-ladder **Art. S**⟨⟩ which is pret⟨⟩ trimmed with ⟨⟩ Satin and lace m⟨⟩ on front and le⟨⟩ the legs being ⟨⟩ widely and tastefu⟨⟩ trimmed with la⟨⟩
In **Rose, Sky, Nil, Navy.**	In **Sky, Rose, Nil.**	In **Rose, Sky, Nil, Ivory.**	In **Lupine, Ivory, Rose.**	In **Rose, Sky, Ap**⟨⟩ or **Ivory.**
Size WX only.	Size W only.	Size WX only.	Size OS only.	Size W only.
Price **9/11**	Price **13/6**	Price **9/6**	Price **13/6**	Price **6/**⟨⟩

SINGLE-BREASTED SUITS IN FASHIONABLE CLOTHS

C 594

In hard-wearing **Navy Worsted Serge.** Reliable quality and smart cut.

Price - **39'6**

C 595

In smart-looking **Navy** or **Brown Herring-bone Worsted Coating Serge.**

Price - **48'6**

C 596

In **Medium Grey** or **Brown** or **Navy Fancy Worsted Stripes.** A stylish material for to-day's wear.

Price - **62'6**

C 597

In finest quality **Navy Indigo** Botany Serge, or **Black Serge.**

Price - **64'6**

C 553

In good quality **Brown** or **Dark Grey Tweed** Suitings.

Price - **37'6**

C 554

In the latest shades of **Brown** or **Grey Tweed.**

Price - **42'6**

C 555

In superior quality **Medium Grey, Brown** or **Dark Grey Tweed** Suitings.

Price - **52'6**

Stocked in the following sizes :

Sizes	3	4	5	6	7
Breast (over vest)	34	36	38	40	42 ins.
Waist	32	34	36	38	40 ins.
Leg (inside)	29	30	30	30	30 ins.

(Not including Turn-ups).

When taking Leg Measurements do not reckon the Turn-up bottoms.

All Trousers are Unlined.

1937

1938

some Fridays, caused Edward, on arriving home, to say, 'There's to be a big wedding on Saturday'. He knew he would get most of his pieces back on Monday.

The late 1930s were heady days for Empire Stores. Its catalogue had developed through the decade to a volume from which a home could be completely furnished, even to such (then) rare items as vacuum cleaners and washing machines. But with the outbreak of the Second World War the catalogue was reduced in size, almost at a stroke, to the proportions of those of the Northern Trading Company that had first established the firm in mail order.

World War Two

It is always a wonder how any large modern business can continue to operate in the time of a major war. There are shortages of supplies and labour, governmental interference, economic pressures and drastic changes in demand. Empire Stores suffered all

OUTSTANDING VALUE IN BOYS' COATS   EXCEPTIONALLY SMART OVERCOATS for BOYS

C 641	**11/-**	C 642	**12/-**
Real good British workmanship turns out this Overcoat for British lads. Heavy quality Melton Cloth. It is provided with a **half-belt** at the back which helps to give snug fit. In **Navy**.		Another high-grade Navy Melton Overcoat, the cloth being thick and soft to the touch. Three large pockets, lining throughout, **half-belt** and inverted pleat. Grand protector. In **Navy**.	

Sizes	...	... 000	00	0	1	2	3
To fit Boy age	...	3	3½	4	5	6	7

C 643	**14/-**	C 644	**12/6**	C 645	**16/6**
Made specially to stand up to hard wear. In Navy Melton Cloth. Three pockets, all-round belt and length just right. Cosy and comfortable. In **Navy**.		This splendid value Coat fits cosily and snugly. Made from good Mixture Overcoating, with belt, pockets, broad revers, etc. In **Brown**.		A quality Coat. In Fancy Tweed. Wears excellently and always is smart. Can be relied upon for warmth and good protection. Half-belt and inverted pleat at back. In **Dark Fawn**.	

Sizes	...	... 000	00	0	1	2	3
To fit Boy age	...	3	3½	4	5	6	7

1938

this, but being essentially a retail business it was hardest hit by the extreme shortages of consumer goods which followed soon after the outbreak of war as the nation's industry was put to wartime production.

For some years Empire Stores had been using the advertising slogan 'Our Catalogue is our Shop Window' and, surely enough, as the shop windows in the nation's high streets became emptier and drabber, so did Empire Stores' catalogue grow thinner and duller. Many of its best-selling lines, particularly clocks, watches, items of jewellery and clothing, had been appearing for decades without alteration of illustration or price. Then, one by one, they vanished, never again to appear. The £1 watches, the 'plus-fours', servants' uniforms, mangles, horn gramophones, ukuleles and gold 'Alberts' were the first to go, to be replaced by items of sterner purpose: 'blackout' material, working caps for women factory workers, portable cradles for air raid shelters and, as heralds of the post-war age to come, trousers for women.

Other wartime difficulties were the stringent rationing of paper

M.322. RIGHT

A delightful dress in 100% Vat Dyed Printed Spun Silk which washes like new. Has DIRNDL waist which gives a fullness to to the skirt.

In assorted coloured Prints.

Sizes :

24in. 27in. 30in. 33in. 36in.

Price :

5/6

M.324. RIGHT

Doesn't she look grand in this dress of novelty printed Haircord. This material is very durable indeed. Collar, and sleeves are piped in material to match three buttons on front. Panel down front of bodice ends in a deep inverted pleat in the skirt. Deep hem.
In assorted colours.

Lengths :

24in. 27in.   30in. 33in.

Prices :

7/-   **8/6**

M.326. LEFT

A really pretty frock in floral printed Spun Rayon, DIRNDL waist, charming frilled collar and pocket make this a frock to be desired by all girls who like to be smart.
In assorted colours.

Lengths :

24in.   27in.   30in.

Price :

4/-

M.328. LEFT

Girl's sweet little party frock in good quality Taffeta. Elasticated sleeve collar and bodice very smartly trimmed with rows of frilling.   Network pocket, two rows of faggoting on the skirt.

In PINK or BLUE.

Lengths :

24in.   27in.   30in.

Price :

7/6

Lengths :

33in.   36in.

Price :

9/6

1940

Modern BABY CARRIAGES

XF 1240. Smart appearance and smooth running are features of this up-to-date coach built Baby Carriage. Every detail is well finished, and a waterproof apron and good brake are fitted. Colour **Navy** with **Fawn** lining. Similar to illustration.

1945

Prices and Special Terms for deferred payments on Baby Carriages will be quoted on application.

for wrapping and catalogue printing and the labour required to handle clothing coupons and dockets. Then came price control and purchase tax and all the documentation connected with them. But of all the problems, selling was not one of them; in those days there were often queues outside any shop that had anything to sell and whatever was offered was sold at once. One result of this was that soon after each edition of the catalogue was issued, each agent was sent a list of items that were 'sold out and unrepeatable'. There was inflation during the war years and the average wage increased from £3 to £5 a week, but in spite of this Empire Stores' catalogue, although reduced to 50 pages, could still offer a two-piece suit for £2 and a lady's dress for 5s. 0d. Most of the garments in the wartime catalogue bore the government-sponsored 'Utility' label which was an official guarantee of quality. In the long run the 'Utility Scheme', introduced in 1941, with its strict control of price and quality, had a beneficial effect on the living standards of the less well off and in time it did much to help the mail order industry, for the guarantee of quality now offered in the catalogue was not something for which mail order then had the best of reputations. Rationing too was beneficial to mail order because customers tended to buy more expensive garments than usual when using their clothing coupons.

Wartime shortages and government restrictions on the use of gold and silver severely depressed the group's jewellery trade, but this loss was somewhat offset by war work taken on by other departments. Bradford Textile was kept busy on various government contracts, one of which was for making replicas of German military uniforms and insignia for the use of resistance groups and allied agents in Germany and occupied Europe. The Birmingham factory made a large number of National Savings Movement badges, and at the end of the war received many orders from all over the world for the replacement of regalia that had been lost, destroyed or looted. Another interesting job that fell to the Birmingham branch at that time was the making of a gold mayoral chain to replace one that had been stolen. Owing to the restrictions on the purchase of gold, the Council appealed to the citizens of Bradford to subscribe pieces of old gold to make the chain. The response was good and 28 ounces of the metal were collected in the form of old wedding rings, brooches and badges.

1945

Rebuilding a business

In 1946 Empire Stores was under the management of Edward Fattorini, who had previously been running the Tyrell Street jewellery shop. He was an expert in jewellery both new and secondhand and well known as a connoisseur of precious stones and antique jewellery. It was with some reluctance that he had left jewellery for mail order, but when his brother Herbert retired as manager of Empire Stores early in the war, Edward was the only available member of the family who possessed the ability to take over the position. But throughout his time with Empire Stores

1946

Edward was never happy, for he missed his work with jewellery. Therefore he was much relieved when his son Joseph returned from the army in 1946 to take over management of the mail order business. Joseph Fattorini recalls that, on his first meeting with his father after the war, Edward said to him, 'I am delighted to see you back home again. It's all yours. Good morning'. He then handed over the keys of the Canal Road building and returned to his jewellery shop.

Born in 1912, Joseph Fattorini joined the family business at the age of 18. He had already gained some knowledge of the jewellery trade through spending most of his school holidays polishing silver in the Westgate shop, a task he found so uncongenial that he developed a thorough dislike of the business. Therefore when he

MAJOR J. FATTORINI M.B.E., R.A.,
LEADING A DETACHMENT OF
601 REGIMENT RA (THE WEST YORKSHIRE REGT.) T.A.,
AT THE CONFERMENT OF PRIVILEGES ON
THE WEST YORKSHIRE REGIMENT
(THE PRINCE OF WALES'S OWN)
5TH SEPTEMBER 1945.

joined the firm he insisted on going to Empire Stores and, by
working through all the departments, obtained a thorough
knowledge of mail order. Then came the war and as a territorial
soldier he was called up to join the 6th West Yorkshire Regiment as

a second lieutenant. In 1945 he was awarded the MBE for 'services above normal duty' and in the same year promoted major. During his army service Joseph Fattorini became friendly with his regiment's commanding officer, Colonel C. T. (Mick) Wells, and this friendship was to have an important effect on the future of Empire Stores Limited.

Up to the outbreak of war Wells had made a notable career in marketing with a London advertising agency, and as Joseph was determined eventually to work in mail order again the two men had much in common and a great deal to talk about. Both were convinced of the coming of a post-war affluent society that would give enormous potential to the mail order industry, and together they planned ways in which they could establish Empire Stores as one of the leaders in the industry. Therefore when Joseph Fattorini returned to Bradford as a civilian his main consideration was to arrange for his one-time commanding officer to join the Fattorini group. Mick Wells' first job was that of sales manager for the Birmingham business, and within six months of starting work he pushed sales above all previous records. By this time Joseph was established as head of Empire Stores and he took Mick Wells away from Birmingham to make him marketing manager of Empire Stores at a salary of £950 a year. The sum of £950 was chosen because Joseph knew full well that his father would never be persuaded that any employee of his could be worth £1,000 a year. Together the two men set about rebuilding a business that had declined considerably during the war. The pre-war staff of over 300 had shrunk to 80 and the turnover reduced to £250,000. The first move was to re-establish the furniture department (closed in 1940) and then, gradually, to build up the catalogue to its pre-war dimensions.

It was not an ideal time to expand a business, for the years 1946–51 were particularly gloomy ones in Britain. It is difficult for those who did not live through those years to realise how depressing they were. The newspapers were publishing statistics to prove that the British people had never been so well paid, well housed, fed and clothed, but in retrospect they did not appear to be so. Many things were rationed: food, sweets, clothes, and even bread (which had never been rationed during the war years). There were serious shortages of fuel and during winter everyone complained of the cold. Above all, it was a period of fear. Nearly everybody thought that the third world war would shortly begin with the Russians sending their armies marching into western Europe, and most were afraid that the atom bomb would eventually go off somewhere. It was not the best time for making long-term business plans but for Empire Stores it was a matter of then or never, for on the credit side a new affluent working class was emerging from the old impoverished one, a class that, traditionally, did not save money no matter what the size of the family income. Miners particularly had come into their own and soon became an industrial elite.

This was the market that Wells and Fattorini were determined to secure, and it was a vast one. And yet the potential expansion to capture a share of this market had to be undertaken with great care, for relying on credit customers (as mail order always has) meant that the cash flow had to be carefully controlled. There was also the fact that, in expanding, large sums of money would be required for increased stockholdings. All in all the firm's entire financial operations had to be handled with great prudence and circumspection.

The first move was to reorganise the firm and put it on a modern, efficient footing. Ever since its beginnings Empire Stores had been run on a rather loose basis as a part of the Bradford jewellery business, without any attempt ever having been made to form a proper management structure. Between them, Joseph Fattorini and Mick Wells created the structure in such a way that its management members worked together imbued with enthusiasm for the immediate growth of the business in a rapidly expanding field. The entire firm was reorganised, and on lines that formed the basis of the highly efficient team of management that today continues to provide the drive behind the firm's development. New departments were formed to deal with cost control, stock control and, most important, credit control. As marketing manager, Mick Wells formed a squad of hard-working, persistent representatives who travelled all over the country recruiting new agents through the time-honoured, and laborious, method of knocking on doors. Then, as the number of agents increased so did the size of the catalogue. Buying agents were sent all over Europe in search of new lines; others scouted the London department stores looking for new imports. In fact 'buying' then was not merely a matter of purchasing new stock at will but of hunting for goods and, as often as not, begging for supplies when they were found. Empire Stores was not alone in this intensive hunt for agents and goods, for there were other mail order companies striving to re-establish their businesses. Thus began the endeavour between leading mail order firms to produce the biggest and best catalogues, and the competition continues today.

Changing the image

There was another consideration to be faced by the mail order companies as the affluent society developed. This was the matter of the quality of their wares. For decades the industry had suffered a bad reputation for quality because it catered mainly to a class of custom that was attracted by cheapness and the availability of credit. At the end of the war those same people were well paid and consequently more discriminating in what they wore and how they furnished their homes. And as they could now patronise the large stores, the mail order catalogues had to compete directly with the high street. In order to compete it was necessary for the industry to start trading in branded goods, a market that had always been closed to it because of the reputation for low-class trade. But if the mail order firms could obtain and sell nationally famous branded goods at the same prices as retail stores, they would demonstrate once and for all that mail order was no longer a low-class trade dealing only in cheap goods but could cater for all and sundry on favourable terms, selling on credit but at cash prices. Thus in 1950 a campaign began to persuade famous manufacturers to supply the mail order industry with their products.

There was opposition to the campaign from the retail shop trade, with threats to boycott manufacturers and suppliers who dealt with mail order firms: but eventually the manufacturers realised that they could not afford to ignore or quarrel with the fast-growing mail order trade and by 1960 there were virtually no nationally advertised goods that could not be obtained through a catalogue.

In 1950 Edward Fattorini, father of Joseph and a grandson of the firm's founder, died at the age of 75. He had served nearly 60 years with the Fattorini group and at the time of his death was chairman of both Fattorini & Sons and Empire Stores. In Bradford he was well known for the charitable work to which he had devoted so much of his time, although his greatest interest was the business he had done so much to develop. He was a man of considerable culture and an acknowledged authority on Chinese porcelain. His two chairmanships were filled by his brother Leo.

The Fifties

Empire Stores' business continued to grow during the 10 years 1949–60 and turnover topped the £1 million mark for the first time in 1953. By then there were over 16,000 'collector-agents' working all over the country served by a staff of 200 at Canal Road. By 1956 the still-growing business was decidedly cramped in its warehouse and it was fortunate that 73,000 square feet of the Midland Mills building on the other side of Canal Road became available. Forty thousand square feet of this building were purchased and occupied and the remaining 33,000 square feet during the following year. This move made it possible to increase turnover further, and it reached nearly £3 million in 1958.

It was unfortunate that the profits from the Tyrell Street jewellery shop fell during the 1950s, from £20,696 in 1949 to £4,264 in 1957. This business had developed into Bradford's leading establishment of its kind and was carrying on a highly specialised and personal type of trade. But for this very reason it required a considerable degree of personal attention from the management which, after the death of Edward Fattorini, was not available, for the directors were applying all their time and energy to building up the mail order business of Empire Stores. Consequently in 1957 the Tyrell Street shop was sold as a going concern to H. Samuel Limited, the chain-store jewellers. Thus it was that the group's last link with its original business was broken after 126 years. The trade of Sports & Pastimes and its manufacturing subsidiary, Bradford

Sports & Pastimes shop

1950

THEY WEAR BETTER – LOOK SMARTER

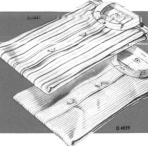

D.4024 Utility. Double-fronted Tunic Shirt, in good quality striped print. Long sleeves with smart cuffs and two collars. In Blue, Brown or Grey. Extra good value. Sizes 0, 1, 2, 3, 4, 5, 6. £1/7/6

D.4031 Utility. Wool shirt, of exceptionally good quality. A warm and serviceable style, with neat stripes in various colours. Long Sleeves. Sizes 0, 1, 2, 3, 4, 5, 6. £1/1/0

D.4029 Utility. Extra good value is offered in this durable Sateen Shirt with smart printed stripes of various colours. Long sleeves and smart cuffs. Sizes 0, 1, 2, 3, 4, 5, 6. 15/8

The above prices include 4½d. carriage.

D.4029

...022 Utility. Smart Tunic Shirt, in good ...ty striped Poplin, with two Trubenised ...ars. In the newest shades of Blue, Brown, ... Grey. Sizes 0, 1, 2, 3, 4, 5, 6. £1/13/7

...025 Utility. Exceptionally Smart coat style Shirt, in the ...y best quality Italian Cotton. Has a well fitting attached ...ar and long sleeves. In self colours—Cream, Beige, ...y, Blue and White. Sizes 1, 2, 3, 4, 5, 6. £1/9/6

D.4026 Utility. Flannelete Sports Shirt, with an attached collar and long sleeves. In check and striped designs, and various shades of Blue, Grey and Brown. Sizes 0, 1, 2, 3, 4, 5, 6. 11/5

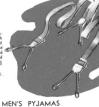

D.5161 Utility. Elastic Braces of a high quality and good length. Reinforced with leather and fitted with plated adjusters. 6/1

Price includes 3d. carriage.

MEN'S PYJAMAS

D.5131 Utility. Men's Pyjamas, of the highest quality Cambric, with assorted stripes in up-to-date colours. Will wash perfectly and give long and satisfactory wear. Sizes S.M., M., O.S. 19/5

D.4040 Utility. Warm and comfortable Pyjamas of heavy-weight Flannelette, generously cut and very reliable. In various stripes and colours. £1/1/0

The above prices include 5d. carriage.

your collar size is	14	14½	15	15½	16	16½	17
...t neckband will be	13½	14	14½	15½	16	16½	
...der Shirt size	0	1	2	3	4	5	6

All prices on this page include 4½d. carriage.

D.5131

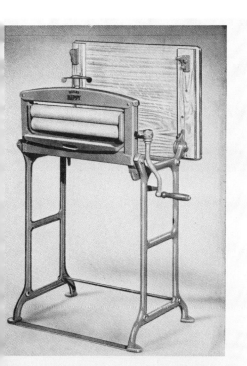

J.9610. The Coronet Cub is an attractive miniature camera, synchronised for use with Coronet Flash Outfit. Streamlined top and Direct Vision Viewfinder, lens barrel and bottom panel in high quality aluminium. Time and Instantaneous shutter, F.11 stop and built-in Colour Filter. Takes Coronet 888, Kodak 828 or Ilford 88 roll film, giving pictures size 28mm. x 40mm. Eight pictures per roll. **£3/18/0**

F.7343. The "Nippy" Wringer is easy to operate and folds to make a sturdy kitchen table. 16 in. x 2 in. rubber rollers, with self lubricating bearings. Enamelled cast iron-frame, designed for easy cleaning. Height, when folded 30 in. Size of table top 23 in. x 17 in. **£7/7/0**

1952

M.1564. Beautifully flared, fitting Coat with soft roll pleats at back and front. In excellent quality Winter Coating, trimmed with black curl cloth. In Maroon or Navy.
Hips 39, 41, 42 in.
Length 46, 46, 46 in.
£6/7/5

M.1566

M.1567

M.1564

M.1563. A fashionable, wide collar gives distinction to this smart Coat of Woollen Diagonal Cord trimmed with velvet. The back, as shown in the inset, has a half-belt and centre pleat. In Rust or Navy.

| Hips | 35 | 36 | 39 in. |
| Length | 44 | 44 | 46 in. |

£6/13/0

M.1567. An attractive Coat, excellently cut and tailored, in high quality Tweed. In various styles, similar to the illustration, and assorted fashionable colours.

Hips				
38	40	42	44	48 in.
Length				
45	46	46	47	47 in.

£4/10/0

M.1566. Excellent value is offered in this stylish winter Coat of high quality Winter Coating. Beautifully cut, in various styles similar to the illustration. Assorted fashionable colours.

| Hips | 38 | 40 | 42 | 44 | 46 | 48 in. |
| Length | 45 | 45 | 46 | 47 | 47 | 47 in. | **£4/10/0** |

All prices in this catalogue include carriage.

M.1565. smart coats lovely high Wool Exce and Pink, Blue,
42
L
46

M.1565

Textile, also declined during the 1950s, and for the same reason — that it was incompatible with a nationwide multi-million pound mail order business. On the other hand, the wholesale firm of E. Robertshaw grew considerably during the period. It was then supplying clothing, footwear, drapery, radios, televisions, washing machines and cookers to hundreds of retailers all over the West Riding. The Birmingham business was also flourishing, having grown to be the second largest maker of masonic and Buffalo order insignia in the country. Its range of masonic items alone filled a 68-page catalogue of medals, badges, levels, chains, wands, swords and dirks as well as a full range of masonic clothing made by Bradford Textile. Short of space in 1958, the Birmingham branch moved to a larger factory on the corner of Harford Street and Barr Street in the heart of Birmingham's precious metal and jewellery trade.

J.9419

J.9419
THIRTY HOUR TIMEPIECE, in a beautifully finished oak veneer case. Chrome bezel and domed dial. An accurate time keeper.

£2/13/0

1954

By the end of the 1950s Empire Stores was supplying some 20,000 agents and there were 20 representatives travelling the country recruiting even more. In the warehouses and offices in Canal Road more than 500 people were employed.

In 1958 the name of the parent company was changed to Fattorini & Sons (Holdings) Limited with a nominal share capital of £500,000. At the same time the Birmingham business became Fattorini & Sons Limited. Also in 1958 Mick Wells was awarded the OBE for his work in resettling Maltese refugees in Britain after their expulsion from Egypt by President Nasser. Later he was appointed to the main board of Fattorini & Sons (Holdings), the first non-member of the Fattorini family to hold a board position with the company.

F.8001. Soundly constructed Bedstead of modern design. Fitted with brackets. **EXTERIOR VENEER OAK** on face sides of panels. Golden Oak or Jacobean bright finish. 3 ft. wide.

Cash Price **£4/19/6**

or 16/0 deposit and 26 weekly payments of 3/6.

4 ft. wide. Cash Price **£5/16/6**

or £1/0/10 deposit and 26 weekly payments of 4/0.

4 ft. 6 in. wide. Cash Price **£6/4/0**

or £1/2/5 deposit and 26 weekly payments of 4/3.

F.7182. COIL SPRING MATTRESS, very soundly built from the best quality steel springs. Slot and screw fitting, to be used in conjunction with the above bed ends. Can also be supplied with rounded ends, to be used with a bed fitted with side irons. Please state which type is required.

Size 3ft.	3ft. 6in.	4ft.	4ft. 6in.
£2/10/6	**£2/13/6**	**£3/1/0**	**£3/3/9**

THE SOFT FURNISHINGS ON THIS PAGE ARE MADE BY THE BLIND INSTITUTE

F.8462. Hygienic and comfortable **SPRING INTERIOR** Mattress. Covered with hard wearing material. Pink, Blue or Green.

Sizes				
2ft.	3ft.	3ft. 6in.	4ft.	4ft. 6in.
£6/2/9	**£7/18/9**	**£9/4/6**	**£10/11/6**	**£11/2/9**

F.8463. Thick Mattress filled with high quality **FLOCKS.** Covered with hard wearing striped material.

Sizes			
3ft.	3ft. 6in.	4ft.	4ft. 6in.
£4/11/0	**£5/5/9**	**£5/19/11**	**£6/10/6**

F.8464. Cot Mattress. Well filled with good quality **FLOCKS** and covered with durable cotton. In Pastel Blue or Pink. Size 46 x 22 ins. **£1/12/9**

F.8470. FEATHER PILLOW, in a double feather proof case. Size 27 x 18 ins. **15/6**

F.8466. FLOCK PILLOW, covered with hard wearing material. Size 27 x 18 ins. **10/3**

F.8471. FEATHER BOLSTER, in a durable feather proof case. Length 4ft. 6ins. **£1/10/0**

F.8465. FLOCK BOLSTER, covered with hard wearing material. Length 4ft. 6ins. **19/11**

F.8467
Fashionable **SHEET GLASS MIRROR** with a hand painted design, in attractive colours. Bevelled edges, polished hardboard back and plated steel chain. Size 22 x 13 ins.

£1/19/6

1954

F.7253
RUBBER KNEELING MAT, with fluted underside, to give a soft cushion effect. Handy built in soap container. Blue or Green. **7/10**

F.7394
Quick boiling Electric Kettle, of **HIGHLY POLISHED ALUMINIUM.** Light in weight yet thoroughly serviceable. An automatic cut out cuts off the current if the kettle boils dry. Heat proof handle and feet. Capacity 4 pints. 230/250 volts.

£3/2/6

F.7256
The "Pixie" **ELECTRIC FIRE**, enamelled in an attractive mushroom shade. Fitted with an approved safety guard. Can be hung on the wall out of children's reach if desired. Length 13 ins. 230/250 volts. **£2/14/6**

Moving with the times

By 1960 the once small, struggling firm that Joseph Fattorini and Mick Wells had come to 15 years previously was a major presence in the mail order business, employing 600 people to handle goods with an annual value of over £4 million. Joseph's confident forecast of a post-war affluent society had proved correct, for during the period 1951-63 the British people reached a very high level of prosperity. All the wartime shortages had disappeared, and although the national economy was shaky and the balance

1968

A An excitingly printed Dress in warm Brushed Rayon. Long sleeved with a front button fastening at the neck and smart contrasting collar. Actual length two inches shorter than stated. Colour as illustrated.
To fit length 34   36   38 ins.
YK 2196   72/9 74/6 85/6

B Turtle-neck Sweater in 100% COURTELLE styled with raglan sleeves. In White or Brown. Also in Powder Blue, Geranium, Royal or Silver Grey (not illustrated).
Chest   30   32   34 ins.
YK 2469 39/11 43/11 52/3

C Skirt waister Skirt in 100% WOOL featuring the ever popular front zip fastening with ring. In Orange.
Actual skirt length
16   18   20 ins.
YK 2194 32/11

D A gaily coloured Skirt in 80% Cotton/20% Orlon. In a modern style with flared skirt and comfortable elasticated waist. Colour as illustrated.
Actual skirt length
16   18   20 ins.
YK 2193 46/9

E Charming TRICEL Blouse featuring frothy lace cuffs and jabot. Neat mandarin collar and back button-through fastening. In White.
YK 2197   Chest   30 32
               31/6

F Stylish Blended Woollen Hipster Skirt with a smart buckle fastening belt. Colour as illustrated.
Actual skirt length 14 16 18 ins.
YK 2198   39/11
       35/6

G Two-piece in ACRILAN/WOOL. The short sleeved top has a back zip and small pocket. The skirt has an easy fitting elasticated waist. Actual length two inches shorter than stated. In Navy.
YK 2199 To fit length 34   36   38 ins.
            69/11 71/9 73/9

page 223

E Boy's Hipsters in Blended Wool with up-to-the-minute styling. Horizontal front pockets, all Nylon trim and zip fly. Smart 1½-in. belt with red flash. In Blue. (See size scale below.)

Waist	25 26 27 28	30 ins.
YC 813 58/11		72/11

F High fashion Hipster style Trousers in 75% Wool reinforced with 25% Nylon. Patch and loop front pockets, all nylon trim and slightly flared legs with plain bottoms. Broad 1½-in Black/Gold belt. Colour as illustrated. (See size scale below.)

Waist	25 26 27 28	30 ins.
YC 814 57/6		70/9

SIZE SCALE FOR BOY'S LONG TROUSERS

Waist	25	26	27	ins.
Inside leg	22	23½	25	ins.
Inside leg	23½	25	26½	ins.
Waist	28	30		ins.
Inside leg	26½	28		ins.
Inside leg	28	30		ins.

HIPSTERS

1968

of payments problem still unsolved, most people, in Harold Macmillan's words, had 'never had it so good'. This remark is often derided but the fact remains that the British were better fed, better housed and better clothed than at any time in their history. Even after taking inflation into account, the average real earnings of men in industry had risen by a massive 42.7 per cent of their 1951 levels.

By 1959 the stage had been reached where it was almost inconceivable to compare the family budgets of the working population with the 1913 example quoted earlier, with its carefully accounted sixpennyworth of material for a dress and 2s. od

1975

FESTIVAL **FOOD PACK** of 67 items with wines and spirit. Comprising: one box of 12 Christmas Crackers, two Rowntree Table Jellies, 10½ oz. "Pan Yan" Pickle, 12 oz. Baxter's Castle Marmalade, three 1 lb. Festival skinless Cooked Hams, 11½ oz. Festival prime Ox Tongue, 4 oz. Plumrose party Sausages, two 7½ oz. Tyne Brand sliced Roast Beef in Gravy, 7½ oz. Tyne Brand sliced Roast Lamb in Gravy, two 1 lb. Plumrose chopped Ham and Pork, 2 lb. Teatime assorted Biscuits, 12 oz. Martin's Shortbread Fingers, two 1 lb. Robertson's Christmas Puddings, 2 lb. Festival rich Brandy Cake in sealed tin, one packet of five Willem II extra Senoritas, 14½ oz. Robertson's Mincemeat, three 6 oz. Plumrose Cream, 4 oz. Sagion Sage and Onion Stuffing Mix, 3 oz. Gold Spinner Cheese spread portions, 7 oz. Ritz Crackers, two 15½ oz. Peach Slices, two 15½ oz. Bartlett Pear Halves, two 15 oz. Pineapple Pieces, 15½ oz. Strawberries, 15½ oz. Fruit Cocktail, two 11 oz. Mandarin Oranges, 7 oz. Terry's Peppermint Creams, 7½ oz. Meltis Newberry Fruits, 15 oz. Baxter's Royal Game Soup, 15 oz. Baxter's Poacher's Broth, 7 oz. Sunpat Salted Peanuts, 8 oz. Riley's Christmas Assorted Toffees, 1 lb. 8 oz. Festival Dundee Cake in sealed tin, two 7½ oz. Tyne Brand stuffed Pork Roll, 9 oz. Festival Pork Sausages, 15½ oz. Tyne Brand Steak and Kidney Pie, 15½ oz. Tyne Brand Steak and

Mushroom Pie, two 7½ oz. Red Salmon, 7½ oz. Festival Peeled Shrimps, 3 lb. Festival whole Chicken, 5¾ oz. Blue Riband Milk Chocolate Wafers, 8 oz. Caddy of Tea, 2 oz. Camp instant Coffee, 7 oz. Meltis Turkish Delight, 8 oz. Terry's Moonlight Chocolate Assortment, 7 oz. Festival Turkey Breast in Jelly, 8½ oz. Baxter's Cranberry Jelly, 6 oz. Goodfare Cocktail Onions, 7 oz. Festival Chicken Breast in Jelly, 7½ oz. Tyne Brand sliced Roast Pork, one bottle Jerez Dulce Sherry, one bottle Haig Whisky and one bottle Taylor's Port.

XF 8845 **£47·50**, 38 weeks at £1·25

FESTIVAL **FOOD PACK** as XF 8845 but without wines and spirit.

XS 8877 **£37·99**, 38 weeks at £1·00

> *Prices quoted are those ruling at the time of printing. For statement on prices see page 3*

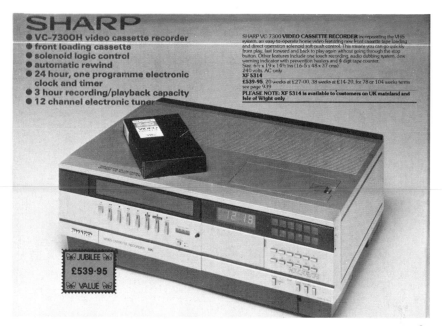

SHARP
- VC-7300H video cassette recorder
- front loading cassette
- solenoid logic control
- automatic rewind
- 24 hour, one programme electronic clock and timer
- 3 hour recording/playback capacity
- 12 channel electronic tuner

SHARP VC-7300 **VIDEO CASSETTE RECORDER** incorporating the VHS system, an easy-to-operate home video featuring new front cassette tape loading and direct operation solenoid soft-push control. This means you can go quickly from play, fast forward and back to play again without going through the stop button. Other features include one touch recording, audio dubbing system, dew warning indicator with prevention heaters and 4 digit tape counter.
Size: 6½ x 19 x 14½ ins (16·5 x 48 x 37 cms)
240 volts, AC only
XF 5314
£539·95, 20 weeks at £27·00, 38 weeks at £14·20, for 78 or 104 weeks terms see page 939
PLEASE NOTE: XF 5314 is available to customers on UK mainland and Isle of Wight only

JUBILEE
£539·95
VALUE

1981

for burial insurance. At the 1959 Labour Party Conference, Hugh Gaitskell observed:

> The recent improvements in living standards have been of a special kind. There has been a particularly notable increase in comforts and pleasures and convenience in the home. Television has transformed the leisure hours of the vast majority of our fellow citizens. Washing machines, refrigerators, modern cookers have made women's lives easier.

And to supply this huge demand for durable goods, Empire Stores extended its range year by year until the puny 1945 catalogue of all that was available in wartime Britain developed into a bulky volume of 600 pages offering a range of merchandise that included suites of furniture, gardening equipment and motoring requirements. The fashion section was compiled through regular fashion shows staged especially for the firm's buyers and fashion experts. The young were particularly catered for, their status and spending power having greatly increased in the immediate post-war years. There was an extensive range of clothing for the teenager, and tape recorders, record players and long-playing

95

records all especially selected by teams appointed to keep up with youthful demand.

The year 1960 was notable, for it was then that the firm was re-formed as a public company under the name of Empire Stores (Bradford) Limited. The new company issued 850,000 5s. 0d shares which were marketed at £1. 2s. each and oversubscribed 11 times. In the new structure, Empire Stores (Bradford) Limited became the parent company of the following:

Empire Stores Limited
E. Robertshaw & Company Limited
Sports & Pastimes Limited
The Bradford Textile Company Limited
Bradford Textile (Sales) Limited
Fattorini & Sons Limited

The governing board of Empire Stores (Bradford) Limited consisted of Leo Fattorini (chairman), Joseph Fattorini (managing director), James Fattorini, Mick Wells and Jeffrey Townson (who had joined the company as secretary in 1957).

One of the purposes of this move was to provide an ambitious programme of further expansion. The first planned step was the increasing of warehousing capacity, and the board had two alternatives: they could continue to buy and equip existing warehousing as and when required or design and build a warehouse to the company's own requirements, large enough to fill not only immediate needs but to accommodate the expected future growth of the business. The latter course was finally decided upon and a search begun for a suitable location. Great care had to be taken in the choice of a site; it needed to be conveniently placed for easy access to both a motorway and a main railway line; it had to be reasonably near the Bradford headquarters and also, most important, in an area where the necessary labour was available. Such a site was found at Lupset on the Horbury Road, halfway between Horbury and Wakefield and not far from Dewsbury where Antonio had launched his business in the early days. Ideally positioned, the nine-acre site was big enough to build the planned warehouse with sufficient land left over to double its size when required. The land was leased from Wakefield Corporation and building started in 1960. The Horbury warehouse was designed with the welfare and comfort of people in mind. Set in lawns and flower gardens it includes a fine modern canteen and good medical facilities. The entire operation of building the warehouse, equipping, stocking and staffing it was completed in a year and carried out without interruption of business or delay in filling orders. At first only soft goods were handled at Horbury, clothing, footwear, bedding, curtaining, etc, while the remainder of the stock was gradually transferred from Canal Road over the following year. With the new, highly efficient warehouse another drive for agents was carried out and their number increased to 30,000 by 1965. Staff increased to 1,500, and they dispatched two and a quarter million parcels that year.

Leo Fattorini, another grandson of the firm's founder and then chairman of the board, died in February 1965 at the age of 81. He had been with the firm for 65 years, having entered the jewellery business in 1900 at the age of 17. He was a well known figure on the racecourses of the north and once owned a renowned string of horses. His place as chairman was taken by his nephew Joseph Fattorini, who also continued in his capacity as managing director.

In 1966 the catalogue contained 17,500 items (one of which was motor car insurance), turnover was more than £12 million, while net profits topped the million mark for the first time at £1,060,000. The figure represented over 97 per cent of the group's consolidated profits, and as Sports & Pastimes, together with its subsidiary, Bradford Textile, were occupying 29,000 square feet of space at Canal Road, it was decided to close the two companies and put the space to better use.

The period 1966-72 was a time of great economic difficulty for the nation. There were periods of high unemployment and much industrial unrest; inflation was having serious effects on postal and transport costs. Then in 1967 came the introduction of Selective Employment Tax which cost the company £35,000 in the first year. The management of Empire Stores countered all these difficulties by continually increasing efficiency within the organisation and introducing new labour-saving methods. The result was an uninterrupted growth in turnover. In 1968, when more than four million parcels were handled, the Horbury warehouse was enlarged by an additional 100,000 square feet.

Much effort was put into maintaining the firm's reputation for fast delivery even when dealing with such great quantities of parcels. This reputation was jeopardised in 1969 through a series of industrial disputes within the post office which dislocated all the incoming mail and most deliveries for many weeks. The effects of the strikes were felt long after they were over, for even short dislocations of the postal service affect mail order business for a period following the end of the trouble. 'Pipelines' become clogged, large quantities of mail and parcels become sidetracked and are only discovered later. But despite this setback the year ended with another record profit through the sale of an estimated 20 million items. In the same year the company's subsidiary wholesale house of E. Robertshaw was wound up to simplify accountancy procedures; all buying was then done by Empire Stores.

The computer age

The 1950s and 1960s were years of steady progress and consolidation as the company adapted to the great post-war changes in consumer demand. Then, throughout the 1970s, it had to adapt itself to far-reaching changes in business management which that revolution had brought about. During the decade, paternalism and individualism in management had to give way to the interdepartmental co-ordination and administrative specialisations that are now essential to the running of a large modern business enterprise. And there was another factor, one that had been taking shape during the previous 30 years. This was the development and emergence of the computer, which has had as great an impact on modern technology and society as did the invention of the steam engine in the eighteenth century. So important has been the effect of the computer on industry in general and upon Empire Stores in particular that a short history of its development is appropriate here.

The history of computing instruments begins with the abacus which originated in the East more than 5,000 years ago. It is still used in the Middle and Far East. For millennia it remained the only mechanical calculating device and was not improved upon until the Scottish mathematician John Napier, devised, in 1617, a system of multiplication and division by means of marked rods (Napier's Rods). Following him, the French scientist-philosopher, Blaise Pascal in 1642 built a successful digital calculating machine, the first to resemble a modern desk calculator. Progress in the development of such machines was thereafter relatively rapid and by 1820 an efficient machine capable of addition, subtraction, multiplication and division became commercially available.

But the computer revolution started in earnest in 1835 when Charles Babbage (1791-1871) formulated an entirely new device, his 'Analytical Engine', which was able to combine arithmetical processes with 'decisions' based on its own computations. The vital element was that the 'engine' was essentially self-contained—ie, an answer computed would be fed back to form the data in the various steps of a complex problem. The key to the working of the machine was in two related innovations of deceptive simplicity but revolutionary impact. The first was 'conditional transfer', whereby the machine was capable of comparing quantities and, depending on the comparison, branch or jump to another instruction or instruction sequence. The second feature permitted the results of a calculation to change other numbers and instructions previously set into the machine and thus made it possible for the computer to modify its own programme.

Babbage's invention was a breakthrough which led directly to the development of the modern electronic computer, the first of which was built in 1948 at the University of Pennsylvania and which used 18,000 electronic valves.

In the year this machine was built, three American scientists invented the transistor, a device which could be used to replace the thermionic valve, and it was at this point that the rapid development of modern computer technology began. This development incorporated the work of the English logician and mathematician George Boole (1815-64), who invented a set of symbols to represent logical operations. These symbols were developed into a system of algebra which formed the basis for the manipulation of rules within the modern computer which give it its apparent power to make decisions. The ultimate effects of the electronic computer on science and technology are too vast to be described here, but one of the first effects of its appreciation in business was that many clerical jobs were taken over by computer. This had far-reaching social consequences.

Computers in Empire Stores

By the late 1960s it had become apparent to the company's management that steps would have to be taken to control wage costs, which were being forced up not only by inflation but by increasing union pressures. In addition, the strong movement towards sex equality led to the Equal Pay Act so that women had to be paid the same rate as men for doing the same job. All these factors resulted in an ever-increasing financial burden at a time when the staff was steadily increasing both through the firm's policy of giving customers the best possible service and the rapid growth of the business. It was also apparent that the ever-increasing staff and the resulting divisions of labour were beginning to slow down operations. There was also the serious problem of recruiting sufficient suitable people in the Bradford district.

Therefore in 1968 the directors decided to instal an IBM computer, eventually to take over the greater part of the firm's vast amount of clerical work, and to house it and its operating staff in a specially designed block to be built in Canal Road. Tony Jacks, the present computer director, was appointed to supervise the installation and programming of the new machine. Within a year he organised a team of 12 to handle the programming and all its problems, and it is to the credit of this team that the first computer systems were in operation by the planned date of December 1970, with a staff mainly composed of people previously employed within the company and trained for the purpose.

Since then progress has been rapid and continuous, and there is now no side of the company's operations in which the computer systems are not involved. The effect of this important development is that since the early 1970s the increase in the firm's labour force has been negligible. Another great benefit is the improved control the systems have given to board and management, particularly with regard to working capital.

Changes and reorganisation

In 1971 Mick Wells was still managing director of the company and Jeffrey Townson (then financial director) and Allen Nichols (warehouse and distribution director) were made joint managing directors. Unfortunately, things did not work out as expected, for by the end of the year Jeffrey Townson and Allan Wade Smith, the merchandise director, left to take up positions as joint managing directors of John Myers, the mail order division of United Drapery Stores. Allen Nichols thus became sole managing director while Ralph Scott, the company secretary, was appointed financial director. Then in March 1972 James Marley, director of agency administration, departed to make a career as a *restaurateur*. To fill the resulting vacancies on the board, Mike Bragg and Keith Whitaker (then senior managers in their departments) were appointed, respectively, directors of warehouse and distribution, and agency administration.

In June 1972 Joseph Fattorini resigned as chairman and took the less burdensome position of joint vice-chairman with his cousin

Joseph Fattorini with Mick Wells

James. It had been 27 years since Joseph's return from the war to manage the firm, and during that time he and Mick Wells had developed it from a small ailing business into one of the best known of its kind in the country. It had been a long hard struggle to reach the 1953 turnover of £1 million, and in the 22 years that had elapsed since that landmark, turnover had been increased to more than £36 million.[1] Joseph Fattorini's place as chairman was taken by Mick Wells.

At this time a decision was made to strengthen the board by appointing two non-executive directors, and in April 1973 John Gratwick, who had over 25 years' experience in management consultancy, was appointed together with a director of the company's then merchant bank. In February 1974 there were differences of opinion on key matters of policy between Allen Nichols and the rest of the board, as a consequence of which he resigned. Ralph Scott then took over as general manager with Mick Wells taking the combined role of chairman and chief executive. John Gratwick was appointed as an additional vice-chairman. It is a tribute to the strength of the company's depth of management

[1] *By 1980 it was approaching £150 million.*

Charles Babbage's Analytical Engine (1870) which led directly to today's computer society
Crown Copyright Science Museum, London

Empire Stores' data-processing plant is one of the most comprehensive in Europe

that throughout this disturbed, unhappy and potentially disastrous period, Empire Stores not only continued to function efficiently but steadily increased both its profits and its share in the market.

By the end of 1974 a new financial director, Don Hale, had been recruited and John Simon promoted to the position of merchandise director. In 1975 Tony Jacks joined the board as computer director and was joined the following year by Peter Fattorini, son of Joseph, as marketing director. Ralph Scott had become managing director in 1974, and he and his executive team reorganised the management to provide a new impetus to the business.

The Great Train Robbery

The fact that the company not only survived the management crisis of 1971-74 but did so with flying colours is all the more remarkable when it is considered that those years were probably the most eventful of its history. In 1971 there was a total strike of post office workers which lasted six weeks, during which time all available car drivers, including managers and executives, took to the road to deliver orders with the result that 60 per cent of the firm's business continued to be transacted. Shortly after this came the 'three-day week' which resulted from the coal-miners' strike in 1973. Fortunately Empire Stores was able to work a normal five-day week because planning foresight had provided generators in all key departments. Nevertheless there were shortages and unavoidable delays.

These troubles, of course, affected the mail order industry as a whole, but fate seemed to single out Empire Stores during its most troubled period for another affliction. This was the loss of goods which resulted when thousands of orders, made up and dispatched, failed to reach the homes of agents: in one month alone, no fewer than 951 parcels went astray. Long and careful investigations by the firm, the police and post office authorities revealed that for over a year there had been large scale pilferage from railway wagons left unlocked overnight at Wakefield goods yard. Fifty suspects were interviewed by the police and many domestic treasure troves were unearthed. As a result, 25 people were charged and nine prison sentences were imposed. In court it was said that the thefts had the 'added thrill of a perpetual Christmas, as it was never known what was in the next mailbag'. The full extent of the company's losses were never estimated but it is certain that at least 500 mailbags were stolen containing between them over 7,000 orders. No sooner had the firm dealt with the robbery and pacified its thwarted and disappointed agents than there was an overtime ban by railway workers which seriously disrupted post office parcels delivery and caused further inconvenience to agents.

Mechanisation

Throughout the years of internal and external tribulations the company was proceeding with building and bringing into operation its new mechanised warehouse a mile outside Wakefield and two miles from the Horbury premises. It will be remembered that the last major expansion of warehousing was in 1968 when the Horbury complex was extended. Since then the firm's turnover had nearly doubled and Horbury was reaching the limit of its capacity. And not only this, but the invoice accumulator system used to assemble invoices at the warehouse was both labour-intensive and slow. It had therefore become necessary to build a new warehouse which would use the most modern methods of assembly and packing and yet operate with a minimum of labour.

An excellent site was found at Crigglestone and a lease negotiated with the Wakefield Corporation. What is now known as the Kettlethorpe warehouse was built at a cost (including equipment) of £1.5 million. The ground area of the building is 216,000 square feet and there was sufficient land left on the site to more than double the size of the building.[1]

In the planning of the new warehouse it was intended that the maximum of mechanised handling should be employed, and senior warehouse management spent months visiting the most modern mail order complexes in Europe and the United States to study the systems used. The conveyor system eventually adopted for Kettlethorpe achieved maximum flexibility of operations with substantial cost saving. All the engineering design work was done within the company and many new and unique features were incorporated into the system. The conveyor loading is carried out by computer programme and the data-processing development team also made extensive studies of systems on the continent and elsewhere. Here again, all the software was designed within the company and the programmes written 'in house'.

It is a tribute to the many managers and staff involved in this complex project that the system was put into operation without any

---

[1] *In 1980/81 the warehouse was extended at the cost of a further £1.5 million.*

technical problems on the planned date in June 1974. As a fitting end to the entire project, the warehouse won Wakefield's Civic Award for the best industrial building of 1973.

Door to door

As earlier recounted, the 1970s were a decade of industrial troubles, many of which had an adverse effect on the company's reputation for quick, secure delivery of orders and, as time went by, it became clear that steps would have to be taken to safeguard that reputation. It was therefore decided to extend the company's own delivery service (which then covered the Bradford area) and to make a gradual change-over from reliance on the post office to a widely spread delivery service of the firm's own. The overall plan was to establish a number of depots in strategic parts of the country to which made-up orders would be 'trunked' and there transferred to vans for local deliveries. The first of these was opened in Bishop Auckland, County Durham, in 1976 and later depots were established at Cumbernauld, near Glasgow, at Chepstow, Warrington and Coventry. Today the company has nearly 200 of its own vans on the road serving 50 per cent of its agents. This development not only ensures that a substantial amount of the firm's business is immune from outside disruptions but it has reduced delivery times to its agents and saves considerably in costs. Another advantage gained from this service is that it creates better communications, for not only can agents return parcels more easily but they can give specific instructions regarding deliveries.

End of another era

In 1978 the last link with the past was broken when the Birmingham manufacturing subsidiary, Fattorini & Sons Limited, was sold to its then managing director, Alan Jones. Although this firm was operating successfully and making a contribution to the group's total profits it was felt that its activities did not fit in with those of Empire Stores. The disposal of this old-established firm severed not only the last remaining connection with the name of the founder of the business but also with the jewellery trade upon which the Bradford firm had been originally founded.

In September of that year Mick Wells retired from the company after 32 years of service. It was fitting perhaps that he chose that year in which to retire, for when he joined the firm in 1946 it was still very much as it had been for decades, a jewellery business with a mail order subsidiary; he left in the year that the last connection with jewellery was severed. During his career with Empire Stores he had seen the turnover grow from £250,000 to over £77 million. He was succeeded as chairman by John Gratwick.

Every chief executive impresses his own personality upon a business and Mick Wells was no exception. Never an easy man to get to know, and uncompromising in his principles, he was an entrepreneur of exceptional ability. He stamped his authority on the business, and many of the sound principles on which it is run today are the result of his sure and instinctive touch. To him the agent came first, a fact that was demonstrated by his avuncular features beaming from the front page of generations of catalogues. One of his most notable innovations was the morning post-conference introduced in 1955 and today an essential part of the company's operations. On every working day the directors and senior managers meet together to read the day's letters from agents. In this way problems are seen as they occur and action taken at management level. Tens of thousands of problems have been thus solved and many potentially serious ones dealt with before they grew to become a danger to the business.

The foundations of the company as it is today were undoubtedly built on the partnership between Joseph Fattorini and Mick Wells which, for nearly a third of a century, directed the firm's affairs soundly and with great enterprise. With Wells' retirement the long association was broken, although Joseph's financial acumen and shrewd mind remained as an asset to his colleagues. However, the retirement of Mick Wells was not only the end of an old era but the start of a new.

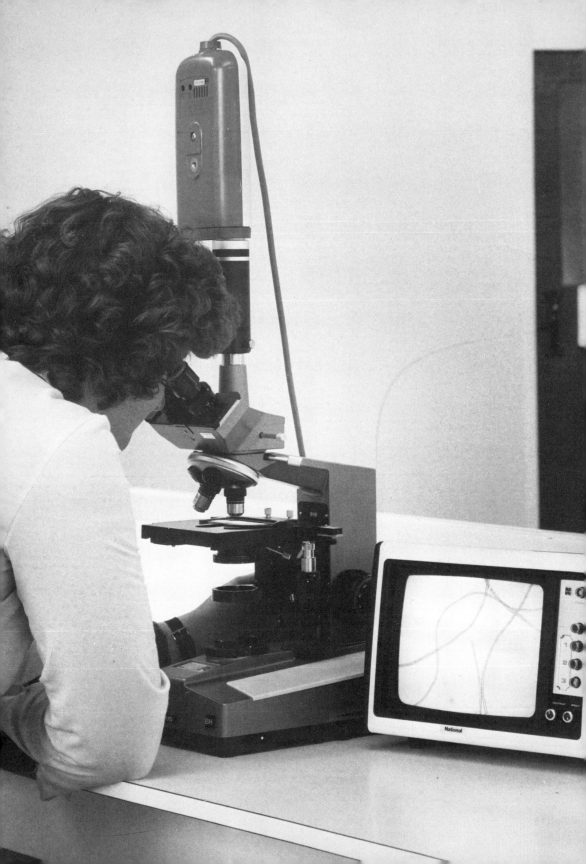

PART 3
Empire in the 'Eighties

The consumer society

Since the beginnings of the Industrial Revolution and the mass production of consumer goods, economists and social philosophers had seen its ultimate benefit as more leisure time for all. But in industrial societies since the Second World War there has been instead a seemingly endless boom in consumer industries, for as soon as consumers accumulate durable goods, these become technologically and conventionally obsolete and, through demand, are replaced by new goods. Thus it has transpired that the populations of industrialised countries prefer to work (rather than relax) in order to buy more goods, and the process of ever-increasing production to match ever-increasing demand has continued to this day.

The growth of demand for consumer goods started at about the time Antonio Fattorini first went into retailing, and we have seen how he adapted his small business to meet the challenge of changing shopping habits and demands. In the 1970s history repeated itself when the retail industry as a whole underwent another fundamental change through the undermining and virtual destruction of the rules of 'price elasticity', which had been considered almost sacred by generations of business economists.

There were a number of reasons for this, not the least being the activities in the USA of the 'consumer advocate' Ralph Nader and his disciples, the campaigns and books of whom, on behalf of the individual consumer, forced a new public awareness that had long been wanting in the consumer society. This awareness concerned not only standards of quality of merchandise but had a profound

LEFT **Examining fabrics for quality in Empire Stores' laboratory** effect on prices through severely increased competition from which no sector of the market was immune. During the 1970s the movement spread to Europe.

The 1950s and 1960s had seen a phenomenal growth of the new supermarkets which had to a great extent changed the face of the retail industry by replacing the small shop. But by the 1970s the smaller supermarkets were themselves largely displaced by the advent of the out-of-town superstores and the discount stores. Just as mass production had changed the retail industry of the nineteenth century, so did mass marketing change retailing by the late 1970s. The great superstores, Aladdin's cave-like monuments to the new affluent society, commanded exceptionally large daily cash turnovers and were able to price their goods at lower levels than were possible for the traditional high street stores. The result was that a considerable section of the public switched its allegiance from the high street to the out-of-town stores which offered the distinct advantages of a comprehensive range of immediately available goods at competitive prices. As an added convenience they provided car parks (sometimes with garage and petrol facilities), self-service restaurants and even play areas for children. But many people do not possess motor cars or do not have the time or inclination to travel to these sometimes remote and often crowded shopping places. Throughout the 1970s, therefore, growing numbers found it preferable to shop in comfort at home, from a catalogue that offered just as much variety and choice of goods as the largest superstore. As a result intense competition developed between the large mail order companies to make home-shopping at least as easy and convenient as a visit to a large store. Mail order has always been in competition with the department stores and the 'multiples', but with the new shopping revolution it became necessary to adopt a more aggressive attitude to the market place. The story of Empire Stores tells how this challenge was met.

The development of marketing

During the 1971 postal strike, the firm's directors and executive staff went 'on the road' to deliver orders. For the great majority of them this was the first time they had come face to face with their customers; but long days spent in the docklands of Hull or among the back-to-back houses of Nelson and elsewhere brought to management a realisation of the company's market, which had previously existed only as an abstract. There was thus created a desire to know more about the customers and to reach a better understanding of their needs. At the same time it became increasingly apparent that the company's public image was not securing the confidence and support that was needed for the planned programme of expansion—ie, whilst the company was successfully creating an organisation to meet the challenge of the new consumer society, it needed a much improved public image which would reflect its new modern approach and attitude to the market. In 1973 therefore a market research function was introduced which became the parent of the present marketing department.

Since the Second World War the company had relied upon a large sales force of full-time representatives to recruit its agents. This method of recruitment is known as 'cold canvassing' as the prospective agent is an involuntary contact who has to be persuaded to take the catalogue. As the company grew it became progressively more expensive to recruit agents by this means, and the law of diminishing returns applied here as in other retailing activities. By the early 1970s all other mail order companies had resorted to advertising for agents, using a postage-paid coupon to encourage prospects to approach them. In 1975 Empire Stores took this course with an extensive advertising campaign in the national newspapers and the popular women's journals.

Recruitment through advertising poses the problem of identifying creditworthy agents. For years it had been supposed that the advantage of the doorstep call was that the experienced representative had the ability to assess the credit risk, but it was found that advertising produces perfectly satisfactory agents and does not increase the number of bad debts. Later a system of judging creditworthiness on a statistical evaluation of prospective agents was introduced, and this proved to be far more reliable than the personal judgment of a sales representative. Progress in this form of marketing has since been rapid and many new forms of recruitment are now used: direct mail, 'drop card', magazine inserts and TV advertising. More than half the firm's agents are now recruited by these means.

As all this was taking place the sales force manager with his enthusiastic sales team continued effectively to 'cold canvas' whilst also adapting their activities to suit the times. The company presents a fashion show at the Ideal Home Exhibition and at other

events throughout the country. All these events are aimed at further building the firm's national image.

By 1976 the marketing department (then responsible for all advertising) was considerably enlarged and Peter Fattorini (a great-great-grandson of the founder) was appointed to the board as marketing director. He had wide experience of the company, having held a number of appointments including those of a buyer and computer systems manager. The marketing department, as well as being responsible for the company's advertising and publicity, has other vital functions. An extensive programme of market research is carried out, new developments are tested and methods of sales promotions introduced. Increasingly marketing techniques are linked with computer systems and Empire Stores is at the forefront of this development.

Alongside all the marketing activities however, the most important and complex production is the twice yearly issue of Empire Stores' 'shop window'.

The catalogue

Of all the changes that have occurred in the company during the last 25 years the most striking has been the development of the catalogue. Until 1955 it was printed by the now extinct firm of Clegg & Sons Limited of Bradford, but the rapid growth of the print order during the post-war years outstripped Cleggs' capacity and Empire Stores went to the printing firm of Watmoughs Limited.

This well known Bradford firm was started in 1888 when J. E. Watmough, a Yorkshire businessman with a keen interest in rabbit keeping, started a magazine called *The Rabbit Keeper*, a title that was later changed to *Fur and Feather*.

Finding the magazine's income to be less than the cost of printing, Watmough purchased an old steam-driven press and produced *Fur and Feather* himself. Other printing work was obtained and a good business built up. In 1896 the firm was incorporated with the cumbersome title of 'The Fancier's Newspaper and General Publishing Company Limited'. This concern grew and eventually established a good reputation in colour letterpress work.

LEFT **Opening and sorting the mail**

The first Empire Stores' catalogue produced by Watmoughs consisted of some 15,000 copies of 200 pages, each printed in colour by letterpress. In the year of the company's 150th anniversary the spring 1981 catalogue is a massive volume of 940 pages in full colour containing 5,000 articles of merchandise. The print run was over half a million copies weighing over 1,000 tons. In recent years Watmoughs has changed over to photogravure printing and this has not only improved the colour fidelity of the illustrations but has helped to hold down printing costs during a period of increasing inflation. Since the beginning of its association with Watmoughs, Empire Stores has been aware of the close co-operation it has always received and it acknowledges the debt it owes to Jack Watmough and Patrick Walker (past and present chairmen of Watmoughs) who, together with their skilled management and workforce, have made an invaluable contribution to the success of Empire Stores.

In 1976 the company established at Kettlethorpe a fine modern photographic studio, fitted with the best equipment, and there most of the staple merchandise is photographed under ideal conditions. Then, in 1978, it was decided that the fashion photography should be done on location: in this way the advantages of natural light and perspective are obtained. The company's photographic teams now work extensively in Europe and the United States.

The catalogue was further updated at this time by the adoption of a new trading symbol or 'logo'. This was part of the campaign to present a more modern image to the public, for it was felt that the old image was somewhat confused and old-fashioned. A firm of international design consultants was engaged and the present butterfly symbol produced. Much thought was given to the choice of subject which, it was agreed, should be feminine and direct in its appeal. The result was a bow or knot (indicating the idea of both a gift and a parcel) tied in the shape of a butterfly, which suggests fashion and movement. The general appeal of the knot lay in its conveying that aspect of mail order which everyone enjoys, the receiving and opening of a parcel. The new symbol appeared for the first time on the autumn catalogue for 1978 and has been since incorporated into all the company's stationery and onto merchandise. It is also prominently displayed on all Empire Stores' vans and lorries.

Empire Stores

Buying the goods

Taken together with 'options' of size, colour, etc, the number of articles offered in the catalogue totals 25,000, and it is the function of the buying department to keep the company's warehouses stocked with this vast number of items in the right quantities, at the right time and at the right price. It is a highly specialised operation, but over the years Empire Stores has been fortunate in attracting first-class buying executives. The company has always cultivated good relations with its suppliers, for it knows that a sound stocking policy is essential to good service for its customers. To ensure this, buyers must have the ability to work co-operatively and agreeably with suppliers. It is also recognised that many customers are employed in the manufacturing industries, and it makes sense to help stabilize that employment by giving preference whenever possible to United Kingdom suppliers.

By the mid-1970s, however, rapidly rising wages in the United Kingdom forced many prices up to a level which produced price resistance, with the result that the company's major competitors began buying extensively in the cheaper overseas markets, especially in the Far East. Empire Stores had for some time been

Packing orders

importing radios, cameras and hi-fi equipment from the East, as well as buying some items within the EEC. To remain competitive in an ever-hardening market the company had to increase its overseas purchasing considerably. Therefore in 1975 the buying department undertook an extensive series of tours abroad with the purpose of finding new merchandise and purchasing established ranges at lower prices. Within a short time a widespread and effective overseas buying system was created. Whilst the company now buys a proportion of its total merchandise from overseas it continues to give preference to home manufacturers wherever price and quality meet its needs.

Value for money

The convenience of mail order shopping demands a consistently higher than average standard of quality in all merchandise, for the customer is aware not only that it is convenient to buy from a mail order firm, but that it is just as convenient to return goods that are not up to the expected standard. A high rate of returned goods is a double disadvantage: it not only reflects on a firm's reputation but increases running costs. A highly efficient quality control department is therefore essential to the running of a modern mail order business. Before 1960 there was little or no quality control in Empire Stores but during that year a specialised department was established to examine all buyers' samples before bulk ordering. The system was later extended to the comparison of the actual deliveries of merchandise against suppliers samples which had been accepted previously and sealed.

The result was a notable reduction in the returns rate, but there still remained a number of returns due to faults in fabrics. To deal with this the company (with assistance and advice from Bradford University) set up its own textile-testing laboratory for examining clothing samples for wearing quality, colour fastness, behaviour during washing, etc. Later, bedding and other household textiles were similarly tested. By 1973 this work had so grown in scope that it became necessary to appoint a qualified technical manager for the laboratory. In time the company formulated its own set standards and gave its suppliers advance instructions regarding fabric quality, styles, size specifications, technical standards and even make-up of garments. Today, Empire Stores' garment technicians work with manufacturers to set the standards and ensure consistency of clothing supplies. Quality control is responsible not only for goods but for the packing of them, for good presentation is an important factor in competitive retailing.

Controlling credit

Customer credit control is one of the functions performed by the agency administration department which is the company's main direct link with its agents. It was this department that handled the massive operation of controlling and directing the accountancy procedure when, in the late 1970s, nearly two million customers' accounts were transferred from an entirely manual to a fully computerised system.

Another difficult and complicated task carried out by this department was the changing over of credit-rating assessments from personal judgment to evaluation through a points-scoring system. This occurred in 1978 after a year of careful evaluation of the new system and the introduction of a mini computer to carry out the work. In computer terminology this machine is 'front-ended' to the main computer and in due course most of the paperwork concerning both advertising and sales force recruitment was dealt with by it. A new statistical department was formed to aid this operation and it is being constantly extended to support the increasing number of functions within the company that require its facilities. Another responsibility of agency administration is the accurate interpretation of the growing volume of trading legislation, including the continuous output of complex regulations formulated by the EEC. In the latter respect it works in co-operation with the Mail Order Traders' Association.

The Mail Order Traders' Association

The Mail Order Traders' Association (MOTA) was formed in 1941 as a representative body to deal with government departments on such wartime matters as clothes rationing, purchase tax, etc. Empire Stores was among the first members. During the 1960s the association grew in scope and importance with the increasing amount of consumer protection legislation that directly concerned the industry. Much of this government interest in consumer affairs affected mail order in ways that were unintentional: laws, for instance, against unscrupulous forms of 'pyramid trading' which could have had an effect on mail order. Today the association studies all the implications that legislation may have on its members and their customers and keeps a strict eye that nothing slips through which may be to their detriment.

In its turn, MOTA is a member of the European Mail Order Traders' Association, the collective representative of all the major European mail order companies. It examines in advance all consumer legislation proposed by the EEC, to which it makes representation where necessary. MOTA is also a member of the Retail Consortium, a British organisation which represents the interests of the retail industry in general.

LEFT **Vans and trunkers awaiting loading**

The Empire Stores' Cycle Marathon was inaugurated in 1977. Its 250 mile course is the longest single-day bicycle race on record. In 1980 Jean Marie Michel won the trophy, which was presented to him by Miss Britain

Industrial relations

The company is in the fortunate position of being on excellent terms with its staff and it works closely with the trade union that represents the majority of them. This is the result of the company's timely recognition of the growing influence of the unions in industrial affairs. The trade union movement in Britain developed greatly during the period following the last war, with the result that more industrial legislation appeared on the statute book between 1965 and 1975 than during the previous 100 years. Furthermore, the unions established themselves among many workforces where they had no presence before.

Until 1973 the company did not have a personnel department and it was the understanding of the increasing influence of the unions that led to the appointment of a personnel manager. It was then decided to recognise formally the presence of a union within the company. In order to avoid the inter-union disputes that were disrupting other industries it was determined to establish a relationship with a single union, and in the event an agreement was negotiated with the Union of Shop, Distributive and Allied Workers (USDAW). Following this, discussions led to an agreement with the management division of USDAW, the Supervisory and Allied Staff Technical Association. The result has been excellent co-operation between the company and its union representatives, with both sides working hard and with goodwill in the interests of the staff. Regular meetings take place between management and union and there are now well-established negotiating procedures.

Who owns the business?

During the 1960s the Fattorini family gradually reduced their shareholding in the business until, by the end of the 1970s, financial control was in the hands of the City institutions, the banks and the pension funds. Indeed, the remarkable growth of the company over the last 20 years could not have been financed from the profits generated within the business, but depended on shareholders' rights issues and on the sale of loan stocks and debentures. The confidence of the City of London, the financial community and the general public are all vital factors in the expansion of a large company, and it is essential that good communications be maintained between the company and its investors. Along with all the other changes that took place in the 1970s was a need to develop the financial activities of the company and to make and maintain the contacts necessary to fund the planned programme of growth. As a result an excellent relationship was built up with the banks, financial institutions, investors and stockbrokers. Great care is taken today to explain fully the company's current policies to meetings of financial institutions, and many stockbrokers with their clients come to Bradford to see the firm's operations at first hand.

There are currently some 3,800 shareholders in Empire Stores, and nearly 80 per cent of the total shares are owned by large financial institutions. The company is fortunate that over the years it has always enjoyed the confidence of its investors, and it is the present policy to increase that confidence and provide a safe and profitable place for their funds.

The board. FROM LEFT **Keith Whitaker, John Simon, Peter Fattorini, John Gratwi**

INSETS **James and Joseph Fattorini**

Today and tomorrow

The factors that have contributed to the continuous success of Empire Stores are many and various, but those of greatest importance can be summarised. First, it has always given priority to the principle of good value for money. Second, as has been emphasised, the firm has always concentrated on giving a personal service to its customers. Third, it has from its earliest days been progressive in outlook and capable of evaluating and adjusting to

ph Scott, Don Hale, Tony Jacks and Mike Bragg

social, economic and technical changes through a competent and enthusiastic team of management.

Last, but by no means least, the firm has always enjoyed a good relationship with its staff, knowing full well that this is essential to the running of a modern business. Empire Stores has been fortunate in growing up in and around Bradford, a town characterised by the Yorkshire grit of its people. In the early 1960s the Bradford staff was joined by men and women in the Wakefield and Barnsley areas. Staff tend to stay with Empire Stores, and at present there are many serving and retired employees who have been 25 or more years with the company.

The continual growth and the very magnitude of mail order today make it evident that the industry has become a permanent and vital component of the economic life of modern society and one which will continue to increase in importance. In doing so it will have to adapt its methods to suit the demands of ever-developing social and economic conditions as it did in its earliest days.

As in 1970 Empire Stores moved into the computer age, so it will have to deal with other technical advances and innovations as they occur. There can be little doubt that the development of viewdata, video tapes and discs will further shorten the line of communication between the mail order trader and his agents, and when this development occurs the company will be well prepared to take advantage of its benefits.

The world of mechanisation and computerisation is, indeed, far removed from the time when Antonio Fattorini first arrived in Britain to seek his fortune. The tiny business he founded has travelled a long road. It may be wondered what his reaction would be if he could see Empire Stores today. No doubt he would be more than surprised to see the size and extent of the firm's operations, but he would surely be delighted that it is doing no more, in essence, than he did when he tramped the lonely roads of Yorkshire all those years ago: that is, making life easier and more pleasant for people by supplying them with things they want at a price and on terms they could not otherwise afford.

Appendices

Appendix 1

Currency conversion table

£sd	Decimal to nearest ½p
1d	½p
2d	1p
3d	1p
4d	1½p
5d	2p
6d	2½p
7d	3p
8d	3½p
9d	4p
10d	4p
11d	4½p
1s 0d	5p
2s 6d	12½p
5s 0d	25p
7s 6d	37½p
10s 0d	50p
12s 6d	62½p
15s 0d	75p
17s 6d	87½p
£1 0s 0d	£1.00p

Appendix 2

**Directors of the company which is now
Empire Stores (Bradford) Limited
since incorporation in 1909**

Edward Fattorini
Edward Joseph Antonio Fattorini
John Enrico Fattorini
Leo Francis Fattorini
Herbert Piero Fattorini
Antonio Fattorini
Joseph Fattorini
James John Fattorini
Charles Thomas Wells
Jeffrey Parkinson Townson
James Joseph Marley
Allen Townsend Nichols
Allan Wade Smith
Ralph Scott
Michael Edward Bragg
Keith Malcolm Whitaker
John Gratwick
John Robert Allan Montague Storar
Donald Hale
John Hawkrigg Simon
Anthony Roy Jacks
Peter Fattorini

Appendix 3

Empire Stores (Bradford) Limited

Profits and turnovers taken from the annual accounts:
January 1961 to January 1980

Year	Net profit before tax	Sales
	£000	£000
1961	371	4,737
1962	451	5,763
1963	533	6,829
1964	677	7,823
1965	824	9,445
1966	1,060	12,077
1967	1,303	15,477
1968	1,526	18,200
1969	1,927	23,828
1970	2,139	26,568
1971	2,475	30,937
1972	2,697	36,105
1973	3,768	39,579
1974	3,516	42,894
1975	3,660	52,147
1976	4,429	60,265
1977	5,434	77,431
1978	6,887	93,344
1979	8,109	109,232
1980	9,121	134,246

Sales for 1973 onwards are shown exclusive of purchase tax and VAT.